The New Loyalist Index

Volume III

Including Cape Cod & Islands,
Massachusetts, New Hampshire, New Jersey
and New York Loyalists

Paul J. Bunnell, F.A.C.G., U.E.

HERITAGE BOOKS
2007

HERITAGE BOOKS
AN IMPRINT OF HERITAGE BOOKS, INC.

Books, CDs, and more—Worldwide

For our listing of thousands of titles see our website
at
www.HeritageBooks.com

Published 2007 by
HERITAGE BOOKS, INC.
Publishing Division
65 East Main Street
Westminster, Maryland 21157-5026

Copyright © 1998 Paul J. Bunnell

Cover illustration by Paul J. Bunnell
Copyright © 1989

All rights reserved. No part of this book may be reproduced or transmitted in any form or by any means, electronic or mechanical, including photocopying, recording or by any information storage and retrieval system without written permission from the author, except for the inclusion of brief quotations in a review.

International Standard Book Number: 978-0-7884-0987-5

In Loving Memory

My Parents

Lorraine Muriel (Violette) Bunnell
(100% Acadian & Quebec French Canadian)
b. 6 May 1925, Beverly, Essex Co., Massachusetts
d. 6 July 1995, Ryderwood, Cowliz Co., Washington

Married
6 June 1941, Amesbury, Essex Co., Massachusetts

James Henry Bunnell Sr., U.E.
(American Loyalist, Italian & Irish)
World War II Veteran of (D-Day Invasion) Normandy, France and the Far East
b. 20 Jan. 1921, Amesbury, Essex Co., Massachusetts
d. 29 May 1996, Marstons Mills, Barnstable Co., Massachusetts

Angels Are Our Ancestors

Can you hear them ... They are all around us.
Can you see them ... They can't be found.
They whisper at us. What are they saying ...
Do they know me ... Was that wind, or them I felt.
Something is there.
Did you feel that, or do you care.
Where are you going ... Stop, we must find out who they are.
What do you know ... What did you say ...
What was that ... Oh, I see now.
They are here to stay.

By Jeannine Marie Bunnell

Sources

DLR - Donald L. Roxby, Huntsville, Alabama materials of Descendants of Captain John Roxby, Esq.

DH - Divided Hearts, Massachusetts Loyalists 1765-1790, Compiled & Edited by David E. Maas, 1980, Pub. By NEHGS

ALC - American Loyalist Claims, vol. I, by Peter Wilson Coldham FASG, pub. By National Gene. Society, Wash. DC 1980.

LMTOS - Loyalists of Massachusetts and The Other Side of the American Revolution, by James H. Stark, pub. By W.B. Clarke Co., Boston, 1907

LMTMPC - The Loyalists of Massachusetts, Their Memorials, Petitions and Claims, by E. Alfred Jones, pub. By Saint Catherine Press, London, 1930.

FLP - Isaac & Daniel Fuller land grants 1816 (F10/93) and 1809 (F09/43) found at National Archives of Canada #MS666, Upper Canada Land Petitions for Niagara. Also probate record of Charlotte Fuller & Loyalist Claims for Losses (#MS727 Reel 24) found at National Archives of Canada.

JWC - Research materials found by Jean Wood Cobb of Lynchburg, Va. and from the Drapper Papers, 1994.

AGD - Research done by Allan Dennison of Acton, Massachusetts, much found in the Vital Statistics in Newspapers in New Brunswick, Canada.

RF - Research found mostly in New Brunswick newspaper vital statistics in Canada for Ron Frazer of Braintree, Massachusetts in 1994.

VNB - Research for Victoria Nan Busk of Hayward, California in 1994 and materials found in Oakland Library (Mayflower society), California and others.

Sources, continued

HP - Haldimand Papers found at the National Archives of Canada, 395 Wellington St., Ottawa, Ontario, Canada K1A 0N3 or at The Provincial Archives of New Brunswick, P.O. Box 6000, The University of New Brunswick, Fredericton, New Brunswick, Canada E3B 5H1, both listed under Loyalist records.

HKC #1 - Land grant listed in The History of Kings County, Nova Scotia, by Eaton, Pub. By Mika Pub., Toronto, 1972. Lists the Parr's grants with others dated 8 Aug. 1795. Donated by Shirley J. Nettnin of Champaign, Ill.

HKC #2 - Land grant of 8,900 acres granted under the seal of Gov. Parr Oct. 15, 1784. Listed in The History of Kings County, Nova Scotia, by Eaton, Pub. By Mika Pub., Toronto, 1972. Donated by Shirley J. Nettnin of Champaign, Ill.

HKC#3 - Land grant of 21,380 acres to many loyalist refugees granted by Gov. Parr. From The History of Kings County, Nova Scotia, by Eaton, Pub. By Mika Pub., Toronto, 1972. Donated by Shirley J. Nettnin of Champaign, Ill..

LNJR - The Loyalists of New Jersey in the Revolution, found in collections of the New Jersey Historical Society, vol. 10, Newark, New Jersey. Donated by Shirley J. Nettnin of Champaign, Ill.

GSB - General Skinner's Brigade muster roll of officers (no date). Found in Halifax, Nova Scotia Archives. Donated by Shirley J. Nettnin of Champaign, Ill.. (This list can also be located at the Canadian Archives in Toronto, Canada listed under military records (muster rolls).

DMR - Muster Roll of Lieut. Colonel Stephen Delancey, commanded by Col. Cortland Skinner Esq. at New Town (location not visible) dated May 1783 (file no. C-8374, p.91) Found at the National Archives of Canada. (names are not very clear because of the poor copy).

Sources, continued

WWRD - Land grants submitted by William Waugh of Riverdale, Maryland found in Rawdon and Douglas, Two Loyalist Townships in Nova Scotia, by John Victor Duncanson, Pub. By Mika Pub., 1989.

LCO - Loyalists settlers of Cornwall, Ontario found at Canadian Archives under disbanded troops, military records.

SA - Sources taken from the Town of Sandwich, Massachusetts, Archives and Historical Center at 145 Main St., Sandwich, Ma. 02563. They are The Percival Diary, pub. By Frank Barrow, The History of Bourne, by Betsey Keene, (much of the list taken from) History of Cape Cod, by Frederick Freeman. And material furnished by Henry J. Perry dated 29 April 1985. Other sources referenced here were: Loyalist of Massachusetts, by James H. Stark, 1910, Sandwich, A Cape Cod Town, by R. A. Lovell Jr., 1985, The National Freeman Papers, by W. L. Clement Library, University of Michigan, Ann Arbor, Mich., Ezra Perry of Sandwich, published by Brownson and McLean, N.E.H.G.R., April 1961 issue.

NF - The Nickerson Family History, which took sources from the St. Thomas Library, British Military and Naval Records (PAC), Nathaniel Nickerson Genealogy, Delancey's Brigade, Estates Confiscated at New York, found at the UEL Library (p.253), Early New Brunswick Probate Records, 1785-1835,by Wallace Hale, pub. By Heritage Books Inc., Early Loyalist Saint John, by DG Bell, cemetery records, various town records, etc. This family originates from Chatham, Barnstable County, Massachusetts (Cape Cod), but later removes to New York and Connecticut.

ML - A Maryland Loyalist Muster Roll from The National Archives of Canada, 395 Wellington St., Ottawa, Ontario, Canada K1A 0N3, record number RG 8, Series C, Volume 1904, p. 24 of Capt. Grafton Dulany's Company, First Battalion of Maryland Loyalists, Lieut. Col. James Chalmers, Commandant dated 11 July 1778 at Long Island, New York. (please note that many Maryland Loyalists settled in the

Sources, continued

Fredericton, New Brunswick, Canada area, a good place to start your research).

NHL - The Loyalist Refugees of New Hampshire, by Wilbur H. Siebert, A.M., pub. By The Ohio State University, Columbus, Ohio, 1916, found at the Nashua Public Library, Nashua, New Hampshire, Hunt Room (Genealogy Research Room) Also, taken from the NH State Papers, Doc. & Records, 1776-83, VIII, 810-12; Belnap, Hist. of NH., I, p. 380-81. And the Act of Confiscation, dated 28 Nov. 1778.

EGRS - Ellis Genealogy Record Sources come from, The Ellis Cousins Newsletter, published by Bill and Carol Ellis of Friona, Texas, Some of The Descendants of William Chase of Roxbury and Yarmouth, Massachusetts, 1983, Vital Records of Yarmouth, Mass. To The Year 1850, Dutchess County, New York Tax Lists, 1718-87, New Jersey Tax Lists 1772- 1822, The Loyalists of New Jersey in the Revolution, by E. Alfred Jones, 1972, The Genealogy of Levi Ellis of Lodi, NY, 1990, family wills and probate records as collected by Chuck Spence of Port Crane, NY.

NJNE - New Jersey Newspaper Extracts, from the New Jersey Gazette 10 March 1779 at Trenton, New Jersey.

NJM - New Jersey Muster Roll commanded by Col. Joseph Barton, Captain James Shaw found at The National Archives of Canada, 395 Wellington St., Ottawa, Ontario, Canada K1A 0N3 and at The Archives of Ontario, 77 Grenville Street West, Queen's Park, Toronto, Ontario, Canada M7A 2R9, listed under loyalist records.

4BNJVM - 4th. Battalion New Jersey Volunteers muster roll commanded by Lt. Col. Abraham Bushkirk and Capt. Peter Ruton at Staten Island, March 1778 found at The National Archives of Canada, 395 Wellington St., Ottawa, Ontario, Canada K1A 0N3 listed under loyalists records and the New Jersey State Archives, Trenton, New Jersey, listed under Loyalist Materials, Reel #232, Vol. 4, p. 1225.

Sources, continued

SJJB - Sir John Johnston's Brigade/Butler's Rangers formed in June 1776. This list was found in "Loyalty on The Northern Frontier of New York, 1775-84", by Dwight M. Turner, and found in Families, Vol. 26 #2, 1987.

DSR - Material compiled by Donna Speer Ristenbatt on the Muster Roll of Capt. Peter Ruttan's, of the 4th. Battalion of New Jersey Volunteers from 1777 to 1781 (20 muster rolls, film #232, Vol. 4, page 2121 - 2159) which was found at The New Jersey State Archives in Trenton, New Jersey

DSR2 - Material compiled by Donna Ristenbatt on Muster Rolls of the Loyal Americans Muster Rolls of Capt. Christopher Hatch, and Capt. Jonathan Randell and Major Thomas Barclay's Companies, commanded by Col. Beverly Robinson in 1778 donated to her by Al Steinburg who extracted them from The National Library of Canada, Ottawa, Ontario, Canada, film # CC-4218 & C-4219. Donna has an excellent page on the Web. "On The Trail of Our Ancestors. Web address: http://www.ristenbatt.com/genealogy.

DSR3 - Material compiled by Donna Ristenbatt on Muster Rolls of Capt. John Howard's Company in the New York Volunteers commanded by Lieut. Col. George Turnbull Esq. And Capt. William Gray's company found at The National Library of Canada, Ottawa, Ontario, Canada, film # C-4219 and CC4218 found by Al Steinburg.

Loyalty Never Dies...Ask A Loyalist

Acknowledgment

I would like to thank the many sources that contributed to this book and made it available. The contents of loyalist vital statistics and materials found here serve to enhance the knowledge of the subject of loyalist studies. Listed below are some of the major contributors who need to be recognized for their helpful efforts. If any have been overlooked, please accept my humble apology.

Barbara L. Gill, Archivist of the Town of Sandwich, Archives and Historical Center in Sandwich, Massachusetts.

Nashua Public Library, Clarke S. Davis, Library Director and Staff for assistance in The Hunt Room, Nashua, New Hampshire.

Donna E. Ristenbatt of Manhein, Pennsylvania for all twenty muster rolls of 4th. Battalion of New Jersey Volunteers found at the New Jersey Archives in Trenton, New Jersey and other musters collected by her for her Internet page, and for giving me permission to share this material with you.

All the contributors, sources, and societies as mentioned listed under the sources' index listed in this book.

My Loyalist Ancestor

Corporal, Benjamin Bonnell, U.E.
American Legion under Brig. Gen. Benedict Arnold
King's American Regiment
b.c. 1744, Possibly Morris Co., New Jersey
d. 17 Feb. 1828, Greenwich Parish (Westfield), King's Co., New Brunswick, Canada
bur. 19 Feb. 1828, possibly Greenwich Parish (Westfield), Kings Co., New Brunswick, Canada
Wife. Sarah (Sally) Jones, U.E.
Born possibly in Bergen Co., New Jersey.

Preface

A portion of this work has been dedicated to the loyalists of Cape Cod and the Islands of Nantucket and Martha's Vineyard, Massachusetts; listing many family members and including much biographical information where possible. Though some of these people returned to Sandwich and other areas on Cape Cod, I thought it proper to list them even though the result was a non-loyalist status (I believe). You will recognize many old Cape Cod names: Nickerson, Bourne, Ellis, Goodspeed, Cobb, Phinney, Chase, Howland, Perry, Tupper and many others showing again how this war split families right down the middle.

The listings below deal with loyalists who settled in Ontario, Quebec, New Brunswick, Nova Scotia and other areas of refuge. I also dedicate a large portion to the New Hampshire and New York Loyalists. Always keep in mind that some of these loyalists could have returned to the United States; like many did, seeking family, warmer climate, better conditions, etc.

This time I concentrated on areas I have lived in, including New York where my ancestor, Benjamin Bonnell once lived as a refugee. Therefore I dedicated much of this material to my past and present homes of Cape Cod, Massachusetts and Nashua, New Hampshire. There is much more material from both these areas as they were not listed in my previous books. As noted in those volumes, a person could be mentioned more than once only because a different connection has not been made. The spelling is how it was recorded so there may be a slight challenge to figure out different variations. I listed variations where found.

"Time Cast A Spell That You Won't Forget Me"
(Stevie Nicks --- Fleetwood Mac)

Surviving The Hostile Elements

My ancestors were hardy historical characters who faced many challenges throughout their lifetimes and down through the generations. On one side, my Acadian French ancestors hunted the beaver to near extinction in North America. They tamed the hostile wilderness, creating many successful farms and villages throughout Acadia (what are now Nova Scotia and New Brunswick, Canada). Later, the English came and tried to force the Acadians out, expelling them to many other locations throughout the world between 1755 and 1790. Because pelts brought such a high price the English took Acadian lands, and decimated the beaver population in order to supply the market places of Europe

After the American Revolution or Civil War ended in 1783, the Loyalists, my ancestors who supported the English, lost their homes in the colonies and had to flee to Canada. In New Brunswick, my ancestor Benjamin Bonnell was granted 200 acres of land by King George III located at the end of Long Reach (Westfield), King's County for his services in that war. Benjamin cleared the land for farming and built a small home which is now the Harding House. It still stands today thanks to the restoration efforts of Howard and Diane Heans.. Beavers were becoming less abundant as the Native North Americans traded them to the English for needed goods.

By the mid 1800s, the beaver was nearly wiped out in North America. The Bonnells of New Brunswick immigrated to Boston, Massachusetts seeking a better life. The need to leave their homeland brought about many difficult decisions, lack of work was now the driving force. Boston was a melting pot. The Bonnells intermarried with the Irish potato famine refugees of 1848. Life was tough for the Bunnells and Kellys, but they came from a strong background. They were survivors.

As the Industrial Revolution swept the entire world, hard pressed areas of French Canada, Maine, and New Brunswick sent people south to the Merrimac and Connecticut Valleys to find work in the factories and mills there. Large French families filled Lowell, Manchester, Methuen, Amesbury, Haverhill, Lawrence, Pawtucket, and other mill cities. By 1900, the French invasion was in full swing, and my other ancestors were seeking the same -- a better life. Reality challenged them again, but their drive for survival would prove them successes ahead.

In the early nineteen hundreds, my final bloodline came to America, leaving the threat of the fascist takeover in Italy behind. The Bertoglis fled northern Italy arriving at Ellis Island, New York. Then it was on to Boston, and finally to Amesbury, Massachusetts to work at the hat factory there. When their first born son received a draft notice from the government of fascist dictator Mussolini, telling him to report to his army, Caterina Bertogli promptly ripped it up and threw it out. This made a very clear statement: now they were free.

My ancestral melting pot finally came together in 1941 when James Henry Bunnell married Lorraine Muriel Violette. This brought together the oppressed Acadians, assaulted Quebecois, refugee Loyalists, destitute Irish emigrants, and the economically and politically deprived Italians: a bloodline of strong fighters who have survived many challenges in the past 300 years.

The test continued after World War II when opportunities for workers of the failing eastern factories opened up in the western United States. Aerospace was a new field, and in California the industry was churning out planes by the thousands, supplying a world demand. This author, though born in Amesbury, Massachusetts, spent 22 years of his life growing up the California way. Yet I always dreamt of the small New England towns and the four seasons of the eastern seaboard we left behind in 1953. Something always called out for me there.

Taking my family out of economic security into uncertainty brought out a strong sense of heritage and survival, a challenge to make it happen. I now know this came out of my heroic bloodlines. That challenge was met several times throughout the years. For 20 years, life was good for us living on Cape Cod, Massachusetts. I found my purpose and history, and I began to write books about it. I wanted all these brave ancestors to be remembered so others would be able to learn more about the past. I also wanted to better the future somehow. My focus has always been on the American Loyalists, but I never turned my back on the other brave genealogical lines running through my veins.

In 1996, my biggest challenge thus far in life slapped my family and myself right in the face. My employer of nearly 20 years announced the downsizing and eventual closing of our profitable and secure plant on Cape Cod. Sending it overseas to a cheaper and younger labor force was the proper thing to do, announced the management, placing 260 people out of work. This was a new trend in American business; aimed at making bigger corporate short - gained profits at the cost of the employee and weakening the U.S. economy. The result being: workers earn lower incomes while jobs go overseas or to cheaper areas. This is the largest conspiracy facing American workers today. Society must stop this corporate giant soon or we will again be a country of refugees.

Taking nearly one year to find work, our lives slowly came back together when we moved into one of the smaller mill cities in Nashua, New Hampshire. Our new home is just a few hundred yards from the Merrimac River. This is nearly the same distance from the same river in Amesbury where I was born in 1946. Right next to the hat factory where my immigrant ancestors started their new lives. I felt that I had come full circle.

Still very much affected by the loses suffered in 1995/6; my job, my home, both my parents, hearing about the death of a close school friend; I struggled to work each day. I was happy to be employed, but still felt a deep emptiness. I drove the 30 miles every day to Welmington, Massachusetts: taking route 3 south from New Hampshire into Massachusetts to route 495 (the road my godfather and uncle, Benjamin Bunnell built and died on 30 years earlier), finally going north to route 93. I drove in the fast lane sometimes glancing over at the blurs of the metropolitan lifestyle I led. My spirit of survival was in question. I felt beaten and wanted to lie back. I didn't want to achieve anything anymore.

One day my attention was taken away from the traffic, to a large marshy area that hugs the Concord River. Not more than 10 miles downstream lay a bridge. At that bridge in 1775 rang out a shot heard around the world -- Lexington and Concord -- the site of the first engagement of the American Revolution. This war sent my Loyalist ancestor, Benjamin Bonnell into battle from New Jersey to New York and to Connecticut, and finally to defeat at New Brunswick, Canada in July 1783. However, it was not that thought that caught my attention. It was the sight of a stately six-foot mound standing high in the middle of that marsh. This was something I thought I would never see in my lifetime.

Surrounding one side of this marsh was a super shopping center not far to the east. To the south was a large residential development. To the north was route 495 and the city of Lowell, Massachusetts. The only natural setting was the Concord River to the west, which made it possible for me to witness a very heroic and brave thing -- the home of a North American beaver. Tree limbs which lay high atop his mound made the biggest statement to nature, and man. This showed the world his will to fight, and to survive, against all odds.

    I didn't believe my eyes. I called the Lowell Parks office and confirmed that the beaver was in fact living there and was protected by law from harm. This startling find proved to me that there is a place for everything ... man, beast, and plant life. If respected, each group can flourish and grow, sharing the wonders of their heritage and culture. That beaver renewed my will to survive, just as my favorite animal, the buffalo has done by returning to the Plains of America. Just as the rebirth and recognition of the native North American culture, which demonstrates a certain respect for the balance and harmony of this small planet, has renewed my will to survive.

    All those mentioned have been persecuted, oppressed, driven out, nearly wiped out, and culturally run over; but they survive, and must live with each other in peace. Canadians on both sides of the separation movement must respect each others' culture and learn to live with one another. Racial and gang related tensions in the United States must cease, and individuals must bring together all the positive things about their heritage and cultures. North America was founded on this type of ideal. The natives of this great land have taught us many things about harmony and respect for nature. Governments must incorporate these principles into their constitutions, and laws; so all natural things will be able to survive.

    A major revolution is coming again. It will either encompass the destruction of mankind, or the rebirth of a world culture that will preserve all the wonderful things on this planet, manmade and naturally created. Great leadership is needed. We need to act now.

List of Loyalists

AARK(?), John
Listed as Private on muster roll of Capt. John Howard's company of New York Volunteers commanded by Lieut. Col. George Turnbull Esq., Commandant at Paulus Hook, February 1778.
Source - DSR3

ABEL, John
Late of Sussex County, New Jersey, listed in inquisition 9 Feb. 1779 at Sussex Court of Inquiry by Isaac Martin and Samuel Meeker, Commissioners.
Source - NJNE

ABLE (Abell), John
Listed as a Private on Muster Roll of Capt. Peter Ruton's Company in the 4th. Battalion of New Jersey Volunteers commanded by Lieut. Col. Abraham Buskirk (Bushkirk) at Staten Island, New York in May and July and possibly August or September and October 1778. (possibly the same person as above?) Again on 30 Dec. 1778 Muster at same place. Also listed on Jan. 1779 Muster (location unknown) and as a prisoner with the Rebels. On March 1779 Muster at Hobuck (Hoboken), New Jersey and again at Powles Hook 7 July 1779 and on August 1779 muster, but taken prisoner on 19 August 1779 and at Governor's Island on 29 Oct. and Dec.1779 still prisoner. Also on 19 March and May 1780 muster (location unknown)(prisoner). On 14 July and 11 Sept. and 2 Dec. 1780 muster at Staten Island, New York (prisoner). Listed on 29 April 1781 muster at Staten Island (prisoner).
Source - DSR

ACHINCLOSS, Archibald
From Portsmouth, New Hampshire. The New Hampshire General Assembly listed him and 75 others as the enemy in Nov. 1778. Thomas Achincloss was listed with him.
Source - NHL

ACHINCLOSS, Thomas
From Portsmouth, New Hampshire. The New Hampshire General Assembly listed him and 75 others as the enemy in Nov. 1778. Archibald Achincloss was listed with him.
Source - NHL

ACKER, Frederick
Listed as Private on muster roll of Major Thomas Barclay's company in the Loyal American Regiment commanded by Col. Beverly Robinson at Guanus on 11 May 1782. He was listed as confined with the rebels.
Source - DSR2

ACKER, George
Listed as Private on muster roll of Capt. John Howard's company of New York Volunteers commanded by Lieut. Col. George Turnbull Esq., Commandant at Paulus Hook, February 1778. Listed again on muster of same company of Capt. William Gray from 24 Feb. to 24 April 1781.
Source - DSR3

ACKER, Jacob
Listed as Private on muster roll of Capt. John Howard's company of New York Volunteers commanded by Lieut. Col. George Turnbull Esq., Commandant at Paulus Hook, February 1778. Listed again on muster of Capt. William Gray (same company) from 24 Feb. to 24 April 1781, location unknown.
Source - DSR3

ACKER, Jacob
Listed as Private on muster roll of Capt. William Gray's company of New York Volunteers from 24 Feb. to 24 April 1781, location unknown. The above Jacob Acker was also listed with him on this muster.
Source - DSR3

ACKERMAN (Ackermin), Abraham
Listed as Private in 4th. Battalion New Jersey Volunteers muster roll commanded by Lt. Col. Abraham Bushkirk and Capt. Peter Ruton (Ruttan) at Staten Island, New York dated March and July 1778. Listed as sick and in his quarters. Also listed as a Drummer on 18 Nov. 1777 Muster who enlisted on 7 Dec. 1776. Again in March and May and possibly August or September (on Guard) and possibly October 1778 Muster at same place and sick in quarters and again on 30 Dec. 1778 and Jan. 1779. Listed again on March 1779 Muster at Hobuck (Hoboken) New

Jersey and again at Powles Hook 7 July 1779. On possible August 1779 Muster (place unknown) and again at Governor's Island on 29 October 1779 and Dec. 1779. Also on 19 March 1780 muster and May (location unknown). On 14 July and 11 Sept. and 2 Dec. (noted as "on board Sloop Neptune") 1780 muster at Staten Island, New York. Listed on 29 April 1781 muster at Staten Island noted that he was "on board the Sloop Neptune".
Source - 4BNJVM & DSR

ACKERMAN, Albert (Allibert)
Listed as Private in 4th. Battalion New Jersey Volunteers muster roll commanded by Lt. Col. Abraham Bushkirk and Capt. Peter Ruton (Ruttan) at Staten Island, New York dated March 1778. Listed as dead. Also listed as a Recruiting Sergeant on 18 Nov. 1777 Muster Roll who enlisted on 7 Dec. 1776. Again on 6 Jan. 1778 Muster at same place listed as deceased on 16 Dec. 1777. Again on March 1778 muster at same place and listed as dead.
Source - 4BNJVM & DSR

ACKERMAN, Lawrance
Listed as Private in 4th. Battalion New Jersey Volunteers muster roll commanded by Lt. Col. Abraham Bushkirk and Capt. Peter Ruton at Staten Island, New York dated March 1778. Listed as discharged. Listed again in March 1778 at same place and as discharged.
Source - 4BNJVM

ACKERMAN (Ackermin), Richard
Listed as a Private on Muster Roll of Capt. Peter Ruton's Company in the 4th. Battalion of New Jersey Volunteers commanded by Lieut. Col. Abraham Buskirk (Bushkirk) at Staten Island, New York in May and July 1778. Was a recruiter, but deserted. Listed again on possible August or September and October and 30 Dec. Muster of 1778 and as recruiting and on Jan. 1779 Muster (location unknown). On March 1779 Muster at Hobuck (Hoboken), New Jersey still recruiting and at Powles Hook 7 July 1779 and again on August 1779 muster in same company and at Governor's Island on 29 Oct. and Dec. 1779 and listed as in the country. Also on 19 March and May 1780 muster (location unknown), on command recruiting. On 14 July and 11 Sept. and 2 Dec. 1780 muster at Staten Island, New York, recruiting. Listed on 29 April 1781 muster at Staten Island.
Source - DSR

ACKERSON, Jacob
Listed as a Private on Muster Roll in Capt. Peter Ruton's Company in the 4th. Battalion of New Jersey Volunteers commanded by Lieut. Col. Abraham Buskirk (Bushkirk) at Staten Island, New York in May and July 1778. Was on Furlow, but deserted. Listed again in possibly October and 30 Dec. 1778 Muster as recruiting country and on Jan. 1779 Muster (location unknown). On March 1779 Muster at Hobuck (Hoboken), New Jersey still recruiting and at Powles Hook 7 July 1779 and again on August 1779 muster in same company and at Governor's Island on 29 Oct. and Dec. 1779 listed as in the country. Also on 19 March and May 1780 muster, on command recruiting (location unknown). On 14 July and 11 Sept. and 2 Dec. 1780 muster at Staten Island, New York recruiting. Listed on 29 April 1781 muster at Staten Island.
Source - DSR

ACKERSON, John
Listed as a Private on Furlow on Muster Roll of Capt. Peter Ruton's Company in the 4th. Battalion of New Jersey Volunteers commanded by Lieut. Col. Abraham Buskirk at Staten Island, New York possibly August or September 1778.
Source - DSR

ADAMS, Joseph
Listed as a Private on May 1783 Muster Roll of Lieut. Col. Stephen Delancey, commanded by Cortland Skinner Esq. at New Town (location unclear).
Source - DMR

ADAMS, William
Listed on New Jersey Volunteers muster roll commanded by Col. Joseph Barton and Capt. James Shaw. Inlisted on 8 March 1777.
Source - NJM

ALGIRE, Martin
Listed as loyalist settler in Cornwall, Ontario in 1790's with 2 dependants, noted that a man and young boy went to Montreal, Quebec.
Source - LCO

ALLAIRE, Anthony
Listed as Lieutenant on muster roll of Capt. Jonathan Randall's Company in His Majesty's Loyal American Regiment commanded by Col. Beverly Robinson on 27 Aug. 1778 (location unknown), noted on Comm. at Loyds Neck.
Source DSR2

ALLEN, Daniel
Listed as a Private on May 1783 Muster Roll of Lieut. Col. Stephen Delancey, commanded by Col. Cortland Skinner Esq. at New Town (location unclear).
Source - DMR

ALLEN, Daniel
Listed as Private who died 30 Dec. 1777 on muster roll of Capt. John Howard's company of New York Volunteers commanded by Lieut. Col. George Turnbull Esq., Commandant at Paulus Hook, February 1778.
Source - DSR3

ALSTONS (?), David Capt.
Listed in Gen. Skinner's Brigade, Seconded Officers (date unknown) at age 43 from America.
Source - GSB

ANDERSON, Jonathan Ensign
Listed as Ensign on muster roll of Capt. John Howard's company of the New York Volunteers commanded by Lieut. Col. George Turnbull Esq., Commandant at Paulus Hook, February 1778.
Source - DSR3

ANDERSON, Peter Ensign
Listed in New Jersey Volunteers under Capt. James Shaw, commanded by Col. Joseph Barton, c.1777. (another listed states 30 Jan. 1777. Another date of 1 April 1777).
Source - NJM

ANSLEY, OSIAH
Listed in New Jersey Volunteers muster roll commanded by Col. Joseph Barton and Capt. James Shaw. Inlisted 26 Jan. 1777, same as below listed Osiah (listed on same muster).
Source - NJM

ANSLEY, OSIAH (Jr.?)
Listed in New Jersey Volunteers muster roll commanded by Col. Joseph Barton and Capt. James Shaw. Inlisted 26 Jan. 1777.
Source - NJM

ANSLEY, Osiah Sr.
Listed in New Jersey Volunteers commanded by Col. Joseph Barton, Captain James Shaw. Inlisted 13 Dec. 1776.
Source - NJM

ANTILL, John Major
Listed in Gen. Skinner's Brigade, Seconded Officers (date unknown) at age 38 from America.
Source - GSB

ARKISON, Charles
Listed as loyalist settler in Cornwall, Ontario in 1790's, infirm and unable to work.
Source - LCO

ARLOW, John
Listed as Private on muster roll of Capt. Christopher Hatch's Company of Loyal Americans, commanded by Col. Beverly Robinson at possibly Haarlem, New York, and on 21 April 1778.
Source - DSR2

ARMSTRONG, John
Listed as Private on muster roll of Major Thomas Barclay's company in the Loyal American Regiment commanded by Col. Beverly Robinson at Guanus on 11 May 1782.
Source - DSR2

ASTEN, (widow)
Listed as widow of loyalist, settled in Cornwall, Ontario in 1790's, but remarks note at Montreal, Quebec.
Source - LCO

ATKINS, David
From Sandwich, Barnstable County, Massachusetts (Cape Cod). Was a laborer. Property labeled for confiscation by the state. Possibly remained behind after the British left. Sandwich records say he was banished.
Source - DH & LMTOS & SA

AWSER, Edward (Sr.?)
Private on muster roll of Capt. Christopher Hatch's Company of Loyal Americans, commanded by Col. Beverly Robinson at Haaelem, New York, possibly at beginning of 1778 and on 21 April 1778 muster.
Source - DSR2

AWSER, Edward Jr.
Private on muster roll of Capt. Christopher Hatch's Company of Loyal Americans, commanded by Col. Beverly Robinson at Haarlem, New York, possibly at beginning of 1778 and on 21 April 1778 muster.
Source - DSR2

AWSER, John (Jr.?)
Private on muster roll of Capt. Christopher Hatch's Company of Loyal Americans, commanded by Col. Beverly Robinson at Haarlem, New York, possibly at the beginning of 1778 and again on 21 April 1778 muster as killed.
Source - DSR2

BACON, Edward
From Barnstable, Massachusetts (Cape Cod). He was denied a seat in the General Assembly or Council in 1777. Possibly remained after the British left.
Source - DH

BACCKUS(?), John
Listed as a Private on May 1783 Muster Roll of Lieut. Col. Stephen Delancey, commanded by Col. Cortland Skinner Esq. at New Town (location unclear).
Source - DMR

BADGELY, John
Listed as Private on muster roll of Capt. John Howard's company of New York Volunteers commanded by Lieut. Col. George Turnbull Esq., Commandant at Paulus Hook, February 1778. And listed again in same company under Capt. William Gray, rank as Corporal. Listed again as Private on muster of Capt. William Gray from 24 Feb. to 24 April 1781, location unknown.
Source - DSR3

BADLEY, Philip Moake
Listed with Sir John Johnston's Brigade and later joined Joseph Brant's Volunteers. Disbanded in 1783 and possibly granted land in Niagara, Ontario.
Source - SJJB

BAGLEY, Thomas
Listed as a Private on Muster Roll of Capt. Peter Ruton's Company in the 4th. Battalion of New Jersey Volunteers commanded by Lieut. Col. Abraham Buskirk (Bushkirk) at Staten Island, New York in May 1778. He was sick in New York Hospital.
Source - DSR

BAILEY, Daniel
Listed as a Private on Muster Roll of Capt. Peter Ruton's Company in the 4th. Battalion of New Jersey Volunteers commanded by Lieut. Col. Abraham Buskirk at Staten Island, New York possibly August or September and October 1778. He enlisted on 11 July 1778. On 30 Dec. 1778 Muster Roll at same place he is listed as deserted.
Source - DSR

BAILEY, Jacob Rev.
Graduate of Harvard College and was the rector of St. Luke's Parish (New Hampshire?). He escaped from Pownalsborough, Maine Oct. 1777 to Boston and then later to Halifax, Nova Scotia. Was the pastor of the Church of England at Cornwallis in Oct. 1779, then came to Annapolis, NS in 1782.
Source - NHL

BAINBRIDGE, Abraham(?) Surgeon
Listed in Gen. Skinner's Brigade muster roll, Seconded Officers (date unknown).
Source - GSB

BAKER, Conrad (Connrate)
Listed as Private in 4th. Battalion New Jersey Volunteers muster roll commanded by Lt. Col. Abraham Bushkirk and Capt. Peter Ruton (Ruttan) at Staten Island, New York dated March 1778. Listed as dead. Also listed on 18 Nov. 1777 Muster at same place as deceased on 11 March 1777. He enlisted on 7 Dec. 1776. Again in March 1778 muster at same place and as dead.
Source - 4BNJVM & DSR

BAKER, Timothy
From Yarmouth, Barnstable County, (Cape Cod), Massachusetts. Was quilty in trial if 1780 of a disloyal speech. He possibly remained after the British left.
Source - DH

BAKER, William
Listed as Private on muster roll of Major Thomas Barclay's company commanded by Col. Beverly Robinson at Guanus on 11 May 1782.
Source - DSR2

BANGS, Seth
Born 1738 in Harwich, Barnstable County, Massachusetts (Cape Cod). He was a Harwich mariner. Had property labeled for confiscation in 1782, later forfeited and was banished from the state. His wife was Naomi.
Source - DH

BARCLAY, Thomas
Listed as Major in his own company muster roll of the Loyal American Regiment commanded by Col. Beverly Robinson at Guanus on 11 May 1782.
Source - DSR2

BARBANCKS, William
Settled at Digby, Nova Scotia and became a teacher of reading, writing and arithmetic to children throughout the area. He later removed to Gulliver's Cove and with Lieut. James Foreman, a high school graduate of England started a superior school in Nov. 1784 at his own home with 75 students. A regular schoolhouse was built in 1789.
Source - NHL

BARBRICK, Benjamin or Benoni Corporal
Served in 2nd. Battalion, 84th. Regiment, possibly 8th. Company or Light Company and served with the British Army in the Southern Campaigns. Disbanded in Nova Scotia, Oct./Nov. 1783. Possibly received land grant of 300 acres from General Small. Property occupied until 1790, which included a house and barn. He had 15 acres cleared, 1 horse, 3 cattle, 3 sheep and 3 hogs. Wife was named Nancy and they had one child in 1785. In Dec. 1811 he petitioned Douglas Township for 500 acres of wilderness land. He had 9 children. He was given the land on 30 Aug. 1811. Another listed but could be same as listed here is for 500 acres at Five-Mile River, NS under Major General Small.

10   The New Loyalist Index 3

Source - WWRD

BARCLAY, Alexander
Private in 4th. Company, 2nd. Battalion, 84th. Regiment at Fort Edward, Windsor, Nova Scotia where it was disbanded Oct. 1783. He was born 17 March 1743, married 28 March 1772 to Margaret............? who was born 15 Oct. 1756. Children were: Catheren, b. 18 March 1776, Alexander, b. 10 Jan. 1780, John, b. 28 May 1786, Robert, b. 15 Oct. 1788, Elizabeth, b. 5 March 1791, Iain, b. 5 June 1792
Source - WWRD

BARETT, Abraham
A Sergeant listed on muster roll of Capt. Christopher Hatch's Company of Loyal Americans, commanded by Col. Beverly Robinson at Haarlem, New York, possibly at beginning of 1778. He is listed as dead on 20 Dec. 1777.
Source - DSR2

BARKER, John
Private in 2nd. Company, 2nd. Battalion, 84th. Regiment at Fort Edward, Windsor, Nova Scotia where it was disbanded in Oct. 1783. On 13 Oct. 1785 he was granted 100 at North East corner bound of land allotted to Major Alex McDonald of same Regiment.
Source - WWRD

BARNES, Seth
From Barnstable County, Massachusetts (Cape Cod). Property labeled for confiscation in 1782.
Source - DH

BARNHARD, Hermanus
From Turloch, Tryon Co., New York. Served in Turloch Militia under Capt. Jacob Miller from 1775-77, then transferred to First Battalion, Kings Royal Rangers of New York. Settled around Williamsburg, Ontario.
Source - SJJB

BARNHAWK, John
Listed as Private who was "taken into Col. Hinly(?) by regiment". Noted on muster roll of Capt. John Howard's company of New York Volunteers commanded by Lieut. Col. George Turnbull Esq. at Paulus Hook, February 1778.
Source - DSR3

BARNSTON, Letitia
Granted with other refugee loyalist's 21, 380 acres by Gov. Parr 8 Aug. 1795 (85?) in Kings County, Nova Scotia. Excheated 14 May 1814.
Source - HKC#3

BARTON, Joseph
Late of Sussex County, New Jersey listed in inquisition 9 Feb. 1779 Court of Inquiry at Sussex by Isaac Martin and Samuel Meeker, Commissioners. Was the Colonel of the New Jersey Volunteers with Capt. James Shaw under him, dated Dec. 1776 to Feb. 1777.
Source - NJNE & NJM

BASS, Peter
Land grant petition to John Graves Simcoe, Esq. 12 July 1793 for land between Long Point and Turkey Point on the West Side of Lake Erie.
Source - EGRS

BAST, Henrich
Listed in Turloch, Tryon County, New York Militia 1775-77 and later in Butler's Rangers.
Source - SJJB

BATCHELDER, Breed
A gentleman from Packersfield, NH. The New Hampshire General Assembly listed him and 75 others as the enemy in Nov. 1778. On confiscation list of 28 Nov. 1778.
Source - NHL

BAXTER, Simon
A yeoman from Alstead, NH (listed with William Baxter). The New Hampshire General Assembly listed him and 75 others as the enemy in Nov. 1778. On confiscation list of 28 Nov. 1778.
Source - NHL

BAXTER, Simon Capt.
Condemned to death by the Whigs, but escaped on the day of execution with the rope around his neck later reaching Burgoyne's army. After the war he went to Fort Howe at the Saint John River, Nova Scotia (now New Brunswick) and settled at Norton, King's County and received a 5000 acre grant there. He died there in 1804.
Source - NHL

BAXTER, William
A yeoman from Alstead, NH (listed with Simon Baxter). The New Hampshire General Assembly listed him and 75 others as the enemy in Nov. 1778.
Source - NHL

BAYARD (Byard), David
Listed as Private in 4th. Battalion New Jersey Volunteers muster roll commanded by Lt. Col. Abraham Bushkirk and Capt. Peter Ruton (Ruttan) at Staten Island, New York dated March 1778. Listed as prisoner by the rebels. Also listed on 18 Nov. 1777 Muster at same place, but taken prisoner 29 Dec. 1776. He enlisted on 7 Dec. 1776. Again on 6 Jan. 1778 Muster at same place and still prisoner. Again in March, May, July and possibly August or September and October and 30 Dec. 1778 Muster at same place and still prisoner and again on Jan. 1779 Muster. On March 1779 Muster at Hobuck (Hoboken), New Jersey still a prisoner and on Powles Hook Muster dated 7 July 1779 and again on August 1779 muster, still a prisoner and at Governor's Island on 29 Oct. and Dec. 1779 still prisoner. Also on 19 March and May 1780 muster (location unknown)(prisoner). On 14 July and 11 Sept. and 2 Dec. 1780 muster at Staten Island, New York (prisoner). Listed on 29 April 1781 muster at Staten Island.
Source - 4BNJVM & DSR

BAYLEY, Philip
A trader from Portsmouth, NH. The New Hampshire General Assembly listed him and 75 others as the enemy in Nov. 1778.
Source - NHL

BEATY (Batty) (Batey), Francis
Listed as a Private on Muster Roll in Capt. Peter Ruton's Company in the 4th. Battalion of New Jersey Volunteers commanded by Lieut. Col. Abraham Buskirk (Bushkirk) at Staten Island, New York in May and July and possibly August or September (as sick) and October 1778 and again on 30 Dec. 1778, same place. Again listed possibly in Jan. 1779 (location not given) and in Regiment Hospital. On March 1779 Muster at Hobuck (Hoboken), New Jersey and at Powles Hook 7 July 1779. On possible August 1779 Muster (place unknown) and again at Governor's Island on 29 Oct. 1779 and Dec. 1779. Also on 19 March and May 1780 muster (location unknown). On 14 July and 11 Sept. and 2 Dec. 1780 muster at Staten Island, New York. Listed on 29 April 1781 muster at Staten Island reported to have died on 22 Feb. 1781.

Source - DSR

BEEBE, Peter
Listed with Sir John Johnston's Brigade and later joined Joseph Brant's Volunteers. Disbanded in 1783 and possibly granted land in Niagara, Ontario.
Source - SJJB

BEEMUS, Thomas
Listed as Private, on duty on muster roll of Capt. John Howard's company of New York Volunteers commanded by Lieut. Col. George Turnbull Esq. at Paulus Hook, February 1778.
Source - DSR3

BELL, George
A trader from New Market, NH. The New Hampshire General Assembly listed him and 75 others as the enemy in Nov. 1778.
Source - NHL

BELL, William
Listed as Sergeant on Muster Roll of Capt. Peter Ruton's Company in the 4th. Battalion of New Jersey Volunteers commanded by Lieut. Col. Abraham Bushkirk at Staten Island, New York in May and July and possibly August or September and October 1778. Says he was on Command in New York and again listed on 30 Dec. 1778 Muster, same place and Jan. 1779. On Muster dated March 1779 at Hobuck (Hoboken), New Jersey and at Powles Hook 7 July 1779. On possible August 1779 Muster (place unknown) and again at Governor's Island on 29 Oct. 1779 and Dec. 1779 with note, "After orders". Also on 19 March and May 1780 muster (location unknown). On 14 July and 11 Sept. and 2 Dec. 1780 muster at Staten Island, New York. Listed on 29 April 1781 at Staten Island.
Source - DSR

BELLEW (Bellyou), John
Listed as a Corporal on Muster Roll of Capt. Peter Ruttan's Company in the 4th. Battalion of New York Volunteers commanded by Lieut. Col. Abraham Buskirk Esq. (location not given) possibly in Jan. 1779 and again on August 1779 muster as a Private and on Dec. 1779. Also on 19 March and May 1780 muster (location unknown). On 14 July and 11 Sept. and 2 Dec. (noted as "on board Sloop Neptune") 1780 muster at Staten Island, New York. Listed on 29 April 1781 muster at Staten Island.

Source DSR

BEMUS, Thomas
Listed as Private on muster roll of Capt. William Gray's company of New York Volunteers from 24 Feb. to 24 April 1781, location unknown.
Source - DSR3

BENEDICT, Benjamin
Listed with Sir John Johnston's Brigade and later joined Joseph Brant's Volunteers. Disbanded in 1783 and possibly granted land in Niagara, Ontario.
Source - SJJB

BENNET (Bennit), Matthew
Listed as a Private on Muster Roll of Capt. Peter Ruton's Company of the 4th. Battalion of New Jersey Volunteers commanded by Lieut. Col. Abraham Buskirk (Bushkirk) at Staten Island, New York in May and July and possibly August or September and October (taken prisoner on 5 April) and on 30 Dec. 1778. It says he is a prisoner with Rebels. Again listed on Jan. 1779 Muster (location unknown except for still being a prisoner. On March 1779 Muster at Hobuck (Hoboken), New Jersey still prisoner and at Powles Hook 7 July 1779 and again on August 1779 muster, still listed as a prisoner and at Governor's Island on 29 Oct. and Dec. 1779 still prisoner. Also on 19 March and May 1780 muster (location unknown)(prisoner). On 14 July and 11 Sept. and 2 Dec. 1780 muster at Staten Island, New York (prisoner). Listed on 29 April 1781 muster at Staten Island.
Source - DSR

BESSIONET, Sarah
Granted with other loyalist refugee's 21,380 acres by Gov. Parr 8 Aug. 1795(85?) in Kings County, Nova Scotia. Excheated 14 May 1814.
Source - HKC#3

BILYOU (Blew), John
Listed as a Private on Muster Roll of Capt. Peter Rutton's Company in the 4th. Battalion of New Jersey Volunteers commanded by Lieut. Col. Abraham Buskirk at Powles Hook 7 July 1779 and at Governor's Island on 29 Oct. 1779.
Source - DSR

BIXBY, James
Was a yeoman from Portsmouth, NH. The New Hampshire General Assembly listed him and 75 others as the enemy in Nov. 1778.
Source - NHL

BLACKWELL, Experience
Sister to Hannah Bourne (Blackwell) who petitioned the Massachusetts House of Representatives on 17 June 1778 to let Hannah join her husband, M. Bourne in exile which was granted 14 Dec. 1778. On this list was Hannah's children, a squaw maid and Experience all from Sandwich, Barnstable County, Massachusetts (Cape Cod).
Source - SA

BLACKWELL, Fear
Daughter of John and Priscillia (Pris) Blackwell of Sandwich, Barnstable County, Massachusetts (Cape Cod) who was listed on mothers petition 17 June 1778 to the Massachusetts House of Representatives to let her join her husband in exile which was granted 14 Dec. 1778.
Source - SA

BLACKWELL, John Jr.
From Sandwich, Barnstable County, Massachusetts (Cape Cod). Was a laborer. Property was labeled for confiscation in 1777. Family was banished and fled to Shelburne, Nova Scotia. He was found to be part of a Tory underground on Cape Cod.
Source - DH & LMTOS & SA

BLACKWELL, Priscilla
Wife of John Blackwell Jr. of Sandwich, Barnstable County, Massachusetts (Cape Cod) who fled to Nova Scotia with her husband was allowed a visit to John's sister, Experience Blackwell while they were still refugee's living on Long Island, New York before the loyalist exodus from that area in 1783. They had a child named Fear. She petitioned the Massachusetts House of Representatives 17 June 1778 to go live with her husband in exile which was granted 14 Dec. 1778.
Source - SA

BLACKWELL, (a squaw) (Wampanoag Native American)
From Sandwich, Barnstable County, Massachusetts (Cape Cod) area living as a maid to M. and Hannah Bourne. She was listed on Hannah's petition to the Massachusetts House of Representatives 17 June 1778 to join M. Bourne in exile which was granted 14 Dec. 1778. (The reason I

list her is that if she did leave she lost family and life on Cape Cod, which should classify her as a loyalist because of her support to this family).
Source - SA

BLAKENY, George
Listed as Private in 4th. Battalion New Jersey Volunteers muster roll commanded by Lt. Col. Abraham Bushkirk and Capt. Peter Ruton (Ruttan) at Staten Island, New York dated March 1778. Listed as deserted. Again listed on 6 Jan. 1778 Muster at same place, but deceased on 27 April 1778. Again listed on March 1778 Muster at same place and as deserted.
Source - 4BNJVM & DSR

BLAUFELT (Blaufield), John
Listed as a Private who enlisted on 1 Oct. 1778 and is on Muster Roll of Capt. Peter Ruton's Company in the 4th. Battalion of New Jersey Volunteers commanded by Lieut. Col. Abraham Buskirk at Staten Island, New York October 1778 and again on August 1779 muster and at Governor's Island on 29 Oct. and Dec. (deserted) 1779.
Source - DSR

BLOFIELD (Blefield), John
Listed as a Private on Muster Roll of Capt. Peter Rutton's Company in the 4th. Battalion of New Jersey Volunteers commanded by Lieut. Col. Abraham Buskirk at Staten Island, New York on 30 Dec. 1778. On March 1779 Muster at Hobuck (Hoboken), New Jersey and at Powles Hook 7 July 1779.
Source - DSR

BOLTON, William
Listed as a Private on May 1783 Muster Roll of Lieut. Col. Stephen Delancey, commanded by Col. Cortland Skinner Esq., at New Town (location unclear).
Source - DMR

BOND, William Sergeant
Listed in 4th. Battalion New Jersey Volunteers muster roll commanded by Lt. Col. Abraham Buskirk and Capt. Peter Ruton (Ruttan) at Staten Island, New York dated March 1778. Also listed as a Private, unfit for service on the 18 Nov. 1777 Muster at the same place. He enlisted on 7 Dec. 1776. Again on 6 Jan. 1778 Muster at same place. Again in March,

May and July and possibly August or September and October (as a Corporal) 1778 Muster at same place.
Source - 4BNJVM & DSR

BOND, William
Listed as a Private (possibly same person above) on Muster Roll of Capt. Peter Rutton's Company in the 4th. Battalion of New Jersey Volunteers commanded by Lieut. Col. Abraham Buskirk at Staten Island, New York 30 Dec. 1778, listed as deserted.
Source - DSR

BOND, William
Listed as a Private on May 1783 Muster Roll of Lieut. Col. Stephen Delancey, commanded by Col. Cortland Skinner Esq. at New Town (location unclear).
Source - DMR

BOOT, Charles
Listed as a Private on Muster Roll of Capt. Peter Ruton's Company in the 4th. Battalion of New Jersey Volunteers commanded by Lieut. Col. Abraham Buskirk at Staten Island, New York possibly August or September 1778 and sick, and again in October Muster. Again listed on 30 Dec. 1778 Muster at same place as taken aboard His Majesty's Ship Foy by James Campbell, Lieut. Of the Marines.
Source - DSR

BOOTMAN, Stephen
Listed on muster roll of First Battalion of Maryland Loyalists 11 July 1778 at Long Island, New York. Enlisted 18 Dec. 1777.
Source - ML

BOSS, John
Listed as Private on muster roll of Capt. John Howard's company of New York Volunteers commanded by Lieut. Col. George Turbull Esq., Commandant at Paulus Hook, February 1778. And again on muster of Capt. William Gray (same company) from 24 Feb. to 24 April 1781, location unknown, noted as on command.
Source - DSR3

BOSS, Joseph
Listed as Private on muster roll of Capt. John Howard's company of New York Volunteers commanded by Lieut. Col. George Turnbull Esq., Commandant at Paulus Hook, February 1778.
Source - DSR3

BOTSFORD, Amos
Agent and member of the land board in Digby, Nova Scotia 1783-4.
Source - NHL

BOURN/BOURNE, Ansel
From Sandwich, Barnstable County, Massachusetts (Cape Cod). Was arrested for being a spy in 1779. His brother was Samuel. It is not known if they remained or fled.
Source - DH

BOURN (BOURNE), Benjamin
Born 25 Feb. 1744 in Sandwich, Barnstable County, Massachusetts (Cape Cod). Died 22 June 1827 in Sandwich. He was a Physician, educated at Harvard in 1764. He was arrested in 1775, but remained after the British left. His wife was Hannah Bodfish, daughter to Joseph Bodfish. She died 24 Feb. 1841. His brother was Shearjashub. Parents were Timothy and Elizabeth Bourn. Trayser mentions that Benjamin took part in the attack on Dr. Freeman. He did manage to stay in Sandwich.
Source - DH & SA

BOURN (BOURNE), Claracy
Child of M. and Hannah Bourne of Sandwich, Barnstable County, Massachusetts (Cape Cod) who was listed on mothers petition to Massachusetts House of Representatives 17 June 1778 to let her join her husband in exile which was granted 14 Dec. 1778.
Source - SA

BOURN (BOURNE), Edward
From Sandwich, Barnstable County, Massachusetts (Cape Cod). Was a Yeoman and gentleman. Family left and went to Great Britain. He was banished for being a loyalist, but was restored by 1790. He was part of the Tory underground on Cape Cod and met at Seth Perry's house (see his listing) with other loyalists and was later banished.
Source - DH & SA

BOURN (BOURNE), Elisha
From Sandwich, Barnstable County, Massachusetts (Cape Cod). Was a Yeoman. Property was labeled for confiscation in 1777. After fleeing a short while he returned in 1777 and left again in 1778 while family stayed behind. He served the British Army or Navy. His wife was Joanna and they had four children. One daughter, Mehitable was banished from the state. He was a former Militia Captain. He stayed in Halifax, Nova Scotia for a while and had reported correspondence in 1779. His house was burned, but his status was restored in 1783. The Sandwich town meeting met to decide his reinstatement. His wife was allowed the entire estate to settle all the legal matters and charges which was enough to cover his debts, but also allowing her to improve the property from time to time (Sandwich Town Meeting Records Vol. III, p.79). He was part of a Tory underground on Cape Cod and met at Seth Perry's house (see his listing) with other loyalists.
Source - DH & SA

BOURN (BOURNE), Hannah
Wife to Lemuel Bourn of Sandwich, Barnstable County, Massachusetts fled with husband to Long Island, New York, visited back to Cape Cod (Sandwich) after being banished, but later returned to live.
Source - SA

BOURN (BOURNE), Hannah (Blackwell)
Wife of M. Bourne of Sandwich, Barnstable County, Massachusetts (Cape Cod) who petitioned the Massachusetts House of Representatives 17 June 1778 for her and her children, Claracy, Samuel and a squaw maid and her sister, Experience Blackwell join her husband in exile. This was finally granted on 14 Dec. 1778.
Source - SA

BOURN (BOURNE), Lemuel
From Sandwich, Barnstable County, Massachusetts (Cape Cod). Was a Yeoman & gentleman. He left the state, but returned in 1777. It is said that his wife stayed behind after he was banished. Sandwich records say his wife did leave, but visited from Long Island, New York, also saying they were banished but returned. He was found to be part of a Tory underground on Cape Cod.
Source - DH & LMTOS & SA

BOURN (BOURNE), Melitiah (Melatiah)
From Sandwich, Barnstable County, Massachusetts (Cape Cod). Cited by town or committee of correspondence that he was a Tory. He was jailed in 1778. Possibly stayed after British left. He refused to take the oath of allegiance. He is said to be the distinguished gentleman whom upon hearing the reading of The Declaration of Independence from the pulpit of the First Parish Church, "trooped scornfully out of the meeting." He was held for a time at the Barnstable goal.
Source - DH & SA

BOURN (BOURNE), Nathan
Was a loyalist and left Sandwich, Massachusetts (Cape Cod) according to Betsey Keene, but returned later.
Source - SA

BOURN/BOURNE, Samuel
From Sandwich, Barnstable County, Massachusetts (Cape Cod). He was arrested in 1779 for being a spy for Great Britain. His brother was Ansel Bourne.
Source - DH

BOURN (BOURNE), Samuel
Son of M. and Hannah Bourne of Sandwich, Barnstable County, Massachusetts (Cape Cod). He was listed on mothers petition to the Massachusetts House of Representatives 17 June 1778 to let her join her husband in exile which was granted 14 Dec. 1778.
Source - SA

BOURN/BOURNE, Shearjashrub
Born 14 June 1746 and died 1806 in Barnstable, Massachusetts (Cape Cod). He was educated at Harvard in 1764 and was a lawyer and JP. His property was labeled for confiscation by the state in Sept. 1775. He was mobbed in 1774. Parents were Timothy & Elizabeth Bourne. Wife was Hannah Doane, daughter of Elisha.
Source - DH

BOURN (BOURNE), Wlilliam
Banished from Sandwich, Massachusetts (Cape Cod) for being a loyalist and he never returned. He was found to be part of a Tory underground on Cape Cod and at a loyalist meeting at Seth Perry's house (see his listing) and banished for being loyalists.
Source - SA

BOWEN, Jeremiah
A yeoman from Dunbarton, NH. The New Hampshire General Assembly listed him and 75 others as the enemy in Nov. 1778.
Source - NHL

BOWMAN, Cornradt
Listed as a Private on May 1783 Muster Roll of Lieut. Col. Stephen Delancey, commanded by Col. Cortland Skinner Esq. at New Town (location unclear).
Source - DMR

BOWSLEY, Charles
Granted with other refugee loyalist's 21, 380 acres by Gov. Parr 8 Aug. 1795 (85?) in Kings County, Nova Scotia. Excheated 14 May 1814.
Source - HKC#3

BOWSLEY, John
Granted with other refugee loyalist's 21, 380 acres by Gov. Parr 8 Aug. 1795 (85?) in Kings County, Nova Scotia. Excheated 14 May 1814.
Source - HKC#3

BOYD, George Esq.
Listed in letters of Gov. John Wentworth of New Hampshire while in exile in Flatbush, Long Island, New York around 1777. Boyd was a member of the Council of New Hampshire. The New Hampshire General Assembly listed him and 75 others as the enemy in Nov. 1778.
Source - NHL

BOYLES, Anthony
Listed in New Jersey Volunteers muster roll commanded by Col. Joseph Barton and Capt. James Shaw. Inlisted 1 April 1777.
Source - NJM

BRANT, Christian
Listed on muster roll of First Battalion of Maryland Loyalists 11 July 1778 at Long Island, New York. Enlisted 3 Dec. 1777.
Source - ML

BRAT, John
Listed with Sir John Johnston's Brigade and later joined up with Butler's Rangers. Disbanded in 1783 and possibly settled at Niagara, Ontario.
Source - SJJB

BRATT, Antoney
Listed with Sir John Johnston's Brigade and later joined Joseph Brant's Volunteers. Disbanded in 1783 and possibly granted land in Niagara, Ontario.
Source - SJJB

BRAY, James
Listed on New Jersey Volunteers muster roll under col. Joseph Barton and Capt. James Shaw, dated 26 Jan. 1777.
Source - NJM

BREWER, Elithan
Listed as Private on muster roll of Capt. John Howard's company of New York Volunteers commanded by Lieut. Col. George Turnbull Esq., Commandant at Paulus Hook, February 1778.
Source - DSR3

BREWER, John
Listed as Private on muster roll of Capt. Jonathan Randall's company in His Majesty's Loyal American Regiment commanded by Col. Beverly Robinson on 27 August 1778 (location unknown).
Source - DSR2

BREWER, Tunas
Listed as Private on Capt. Jonathan Randall's muster roll in His Majesty's Loyal American Regiment commanded by Col. Beverly Robinson on 27 August 1778 (location unknown), but noted to be on Comm. at Loyds Neck.

BRICKMAN, Renard
Listed in Muster Roll of Capt. Peter Ruttan's Company in the 4th. Battalion of New Jersey Volunteers commanded by Lieut. Col. Abraham Bushkirk at Staten Island, New York. He was listed as a Corporal and sick in General Hospital.
Source - DSR

BRIGGS, William
Listed as Private on muster roll (noted, "detached with certificate") of Capt. John Howard's company of New York Volunteers commanded by Lieut. Col. George Turnbull Esq., Commandant at Paulus Hook, February 1778.
Source - DSR3

BRIGHAM(?), Henry
Listed as a Sergeant in May 1783 Muster Roll of Lieut. Col. Stephen Delancey, commanded by Col. Cortland Skinner, Esq. at New Town (location unclear).
Source - DMR

BRIGHT, Philip
Listed as Private on muster roll of Major Thomas Barclay's company in the Loyal American Regiment commanded by Col. Beverly Robinson at Guanus on 11 May 1782.
Source - DSR2

BRITAIN, James
Listed on New Jersey Volunteers muster roll commanded by Col. Joseph Barton and Capt. James Shaw, dated 26 Jan. 1777.
Source - NJM

BRITT, John
Listed as a Private on Muster Roll of Capt. Peter Ruttan's Company in the 4th. Battalion of New Jersey Volunteers commanded by Lieut. Col. Abraham Buskirk Esq. (place not given) in possibly Jan. 1779. Listed again on 2 Dec. 1780 muster at Staten Island, New York as a Corporal. On 29 April 1781 muster at Staten Island.
Source - DSR

BRITTAIN, Joseph
Listed as Ensign in May 1783 Muster Roll of Lieut. Col. Stephen Delancey, commanded by Col. Cortland Shinner Esq. at New Town (location unknown).
Source - DMR

BROOKS, John
Listed on the New Hampshire act of confiscation list on 28 Nov. 1778.
Source - NHL

BROWN, Daniel Major
Listed in Gen. Skinner's Brigade muster roll of Seconded Officers (date unknown) at age 44 from America.
Source - GSB

BROWN, Finley, Capt.
Granted with other refugee loyalist's 21, 380 acres by Gov. Parr 8 Aug. 1795 (85?) in Kings County, Nova Scotia.
Source - HKC#3

BROWN, Jacob
A trader from New Market, NH. The New Hampshire General Assembly listed him and 75 others as the enemy in Nov. 1778.
Source - NHL

BROWN, John
From Sandwich, Barnstable County, Massachusetts (Cape Cod). He was arrested in 1776, but is believed to have stayed after the British left.
Source - DH

BROWN, John Sr.
Listed on muster roll of First Battalion of Maryland Loyalists 11 July 1778 at Long Island, New York. Enlisted 13 Nov. 1777.
Source - ML

BROWN, John Jr.
Listed on muster roll of First Battalion of Maryland Loyalists 11 July 1778 at Long Island, New York. Enlisted 11 April 1778.
Source - ML

BROWN, Meltiah
From Sandwich, Barnstable County, Massachusetts (Cape Cod). He was jailed in 1778, but chose to stay after the British left.
Source - DH

BROWN, Nathan
Listed with Sir John Johnston's Brigade and later joined Joseph Brant's Volunteers. Disbanded in 1783 and possibly granted land in Niagara, Ontario.
Source - SJJB

BROWN, Nathan
Listed as Private on muster roll of Capt. William Gray's company of New York Volunteers from 24 Feb. to 24 April 1781, location unknown.
Source - DSR3

BROWN, Thomas
Listed as Private on muster roll of Capt. William Gray's company of New York Volunteers from 24 Feb. to 24 April 1781, location unknown.
Source - DSR3

BROWN, Thomas
Listed as Private in the General Hospital on muster roll of Capt. William Gray's company of New York Volunteers from 24 Feb. to 24 April 1781, location unknown. The above Thomas was listed on same muster.
Source - DSR3

BROWN, William Sargent
Listed on muster roll of First Battalion of Maryland Loyalists 11 July 1778 at Long Island, New York. Enlisted 12 Dec. 1777.
Source - ML

BROWN, William
Listed in muster roll of First Battalion of Maryland Loyalists 11 July 1778 at Long Island, New York. Enlisted 9 Feb. 1778.
Source - ML

BROWNE, Nathan
Listed as Private on muster roll of Capt. John Howard's company of New York Volunteers commanded by Lieut. Col. George Turnbull Esq., Commandant at Paulus Hook, February 1778.
Source - DSR3

BROWNE (Brown), William
Listed as a Private on Muster Roll of Capt. Peter Rutton's Company in the 4th. Battalion of New Jersey Volunteers commanded by Lieut. Col. Abraham Buskirk at Staten Island, New York on 30 Dec. 1778, the same day he enlisted. Listed again on Jan. 1779 (location unknown) as a prisoner with the Rebels. On March 1779 Muster at Hobuck (Hoboken), New Jersey and at Powles Hook 7 July 1779 and again on August 1779 muster, but still listed as a prisoner and at Governor's Island on 29 Oct. and Dec. 1779 still prisoner. Also on 19 March and May 1780 muster (location unknown)(prisoner). On 14 July and 11 Sept. and 2 Dec. 1780 muster at Staten Island, New York (prisoner). Listed on 29 April 1781 muster at Staten Island.
Source - DSR

BRUCE (Bruse), Frederick
Listed as Private in 4th. Battalion New Jersey Volunteers muster roll commanded by Lt. Col. Abraham Bushkirk and Capt. Peter Ruton (Ruttan) at Staten Island, New York dated March 1778. Listed as sick in New York. Also listed on 18 Nov. 1777 Muster at Staten Island, New York stating that he inlisted on 22 Jan. 1777. Again on 6 Jan. 1778 Muster at same place, but sick in General Hospital. Again in March (sick in New York) and May and July (sick on Staten Island)1778 Muster at same place and possibly August or September and October1778 and again on 30 Dec. 1778. Listed again on Muster dated Jan. 1779 (location unknown) and as a prisoner with the Rebels. On March 1779 Muster at Hobuck (Hoboken), New Jersey and at Powles Hook 7 July 1779 and again on August 1779 muster, still a prisoner and at Governor's Island on 29 Oct. and Dec. 1779 still prisoner. Also on 19 March and May 1780 muster (location unknown)(prisoner) On 14 July and 11 Sept. and 2 Dec. 1780 muster at Staten Island, New York (prisoner). Listed on 29 April 1781 muster at Staten Island (as a prisoner).
Source - 4BNJVM & DSR

BRUCE, George
Listed as Private in 4th. Battalion New Jersey Volunteers muster roll commanded by Lt. Col. Abraham Bushkirk and Capt. Peter Ruton (Ruttan) at Staten Island, New York dated March 1778. Listed as sick and in his quarters. Also listed on 18 Nov. 1777 Muster at Staten Island, New York stated that he inlisted on 7 Dec. 1776. Again on 6 Jan. 1778 Muster at same place. Again in March 1778 muster at same place and sick in quarters.
Source - 4BNJVM & DSR

BRUCE (Bruse)(Brush), John
Listed as Private in 4th. Battalion New Jersey Volunteers muster roll commanded by Lt. Col. Abraham Bushkirk and Capt. Peter Ruton (Ruttan) at Staten Island, New York dated March 1778. Listed as sick in New York. Also listed on 18 Nov. 1777 Staten Island, New York Muster as inlisting on 22 Jan. 1777. Again on 6 Jan. 1778 Muster at same place, but sick in General Hospital. Again in March (sick in General Hospital in New York) and May and July (sick in New York Hospital) 1778 Muster at same place and possibly August or September listed as on Furlow in New York. Again on 30 Dec. 1778 Muster at same place as recruiting.
Source - 4BNJVM & DSR

BRUDENELL, Edward W. Rev.
Served on land board for Digby, Nova Scotia 1783-4.
Source - NHL

BRUSH, Crean
Of Cumberland County, New York. Listed on the New Hampshire act of confiscation list 28 Nov. 1778.
Source - NHL

BUCK, George
Listed as loyalist settler in Cornwall, Ontario in 1790's alone on his land.
Source - LCO

BUMPUS, Marcy
Wife of Thomas Bumpus of Sandwich, Barnstable County, Massachusetts (Cape Cod), who petitioned the Massachusetts House of Representetives 17 June 1778 to let her join her husband in exile which was granted 14 Dec. 1778.
Source - SA

BUMPUS (BUMPAS), Thomas
From Sandwich, Barnstable County, Massachusetts (Cape Cod). Was a Yeoman. Cited by Town or Committee of Correspondence listing him as a Tory in 1778. His Barnstable property was sold in 1780 and was banished from the state. It is believed that his wife stayed behind. Sandwich records say he was banished as mentioned by Betsey Keene and then referred to again in 1783 that if his house was sold that his widow Mercy would become a town charge so the decision was postponed. Obviously from the mention of his wife being a widow places Thomas death before 1783? He was found to be part of a Tory underground on Cape Cod.
Source - DH & SA

BURN, Patrick
Mariner. New Hampshire General Assembly listed him and 75 others as the enemy in Nov. 1778.
Source - NHL

BUSCH, William
Listed in Turloch, Tryon County, New York Militia 1775-77 and later in the Butler's Rangers.
Source - SJJB

BUSH, Benjamin
Listed as Private in 4th. Battalion New Jersey Volunteers muster roll commanded by Lt. Col. Abraham Bushkirk and Capt. Peter Ruton (Ruttan) at Staten Island, New York dated March 1778. Listed as dead. Also listed on 18 Nov. 1777 Muster at Staten Island, New York stating that he enlisted on 10 March 1777. Again on 6 Jan. 1778 Muster at same place, but deceased on 25 Dec. 1777. Again in March 1778 muster at same place and as dead.
Source - 4BNJVM & DSR

BUTCOTT, John
Late of Sussex County, New Jersey in inquisition 9 Feb. 1779 at Court of inquiry at Sussex by Isaac Martin and Samuel Meeker, Commissioners.
Source - NJNE

BUTLER, Edmund
Granted with other refugee loyalist's 21, 380 acres by Gov. Parr 8 Aug. 1795 (85?) in Kings County, Nova Scotia.
Source - HKC#3

BUTLER, Gillam
Listed as a loyalist and merchant from Portsmouth, New Hampshire. The New Hampshire General Assembly listed him and 75 others as the enemy in Nov. 1778.
Source - NHL

BUTT, Charles
Listed as a Private on Muster Roll in Capt. Peter Ruton's Company in the 4th. Battalion of New Jersey Volunteers commanded by Lieut. Col. Abraham Buskirk (Bushkirk) at Staten Island, New York in July 1778.
Source - DSR

BYNGHAM, John
Listed as Private on muster roll of Capt. John Howard's company of New York Volunteers commanded by Lieut. Col. George Turnbull Esq., Commandant at Paulus Hook, February 1778.
Source - DSR3

CALEF, Joseph
From Falmouth, Barnstable County, Massachusetts (Cape Cod)?. He was exiled to Canada.
Source - DH

CALLEHAN, Dennis Drummer
Listed on muster roll of First Battalion of Maryland Loyalists 11 July 1778 at Long Island, New York. Enlisted 27 Nov. 1777.
Source - ML

CAMPBELL, Duncan
Heirs of Duncan granted 500 acres in Rawdon/Douglas, Nova Scotia under Major General Small.
Source - WWRD

CAMPBELL, Robert
Listed as a Private on May 1783 Muster Roll of Lieut. Col. Stephen Delancey, commanded by Col. Cortland Skinner Esq. at New Town (location unclear).
Source - DMR

CAPIBOLT, Robert
Listed on muster roll of First Battalion of Maryland Loyalists 11 July 1778 at Long Island, New York. Enlisted 14 Dec. 1777.
Source - ML

CARNEY, Alexander
Listed on May 1783 Muster Roll of Lieut. Col. Stephen Delancey, commanded by Col. Cortland Skinner Esq. at New Town (location unclear). He was listed as a Sergeant.
Source - DMR

CARNEY, John
Granted 500 acres in Rawdon/Douglas, Nova Scotia under Major General Small.
Source - WWRD

CARPENTER, William
Listed as Private "In Command" on muster roll of Capt. John Howard's company of New York Volunteers commanded by Lieut. Col. George Turnbull Esq., Commandant at Paulus Hook, February 1778.
Source - DSR3

CARRIER, Alexander
Listed in New Jersey Volunteers muster roll commanded under Col. Joseph Barton and Capt. James Shaw dated 12 March 1777.
Source - NJM

CARROL, James
Listed on muster roll of First Battalion of Maryland Loyalists 11 July 1778 at Long Island, New York. Enlisted 13 Nov. 1777.
Source - ML

CARROL, John
Listed on muster roll of First Battalion of Maryland Loyalists 11 July 1778 at Long Island, New York. Enlisted 18 Dec. 1777.
Source - ML

CARROL, Thomas
Listed on muster roll of First Battalion of Maryland Loyalists 11 July 1778 at Long Island, New York. Enlisted 18 Dec. 1777.
Source - ML

CARTER, David
Listed as Private on muster roll of Capt. John Howard's company of New York Volunteers commanded by Lieut. Col. George Turnbull Esq., Commandant at Paulus Hook, February 1778.
Source - DSR3

CARTER, Frederick
Listed as Private on muster roll of Major Thomas Barclay's company in the Loyal American Regiment commanded by Col. Beverly Robinson at Guanus on 11 May 1782.
Source - DSR2

CARTWRIGHT, John
Listed in land grant with others to John Graves Simcoe, Esq. 12 July 1793 for land located between Long Point and Turkey Point on the West Side of Lake Erie.
Source - EGRS

CASHOW (Hishaw?), Henry
Listed as Private, on duty on muster roll of Capt. John Howard's company of New York Volunteers commanded by Lieut. Col. George Turnbull Esq., Commandant at Paulus Hook, February 1778.
Source - DSR3

CASLEMAN, Tetrich
Listed in Turloch, Tryon County, New York Militia 1775-77 and later in Butler's Rangers.
Source - SJJB

CASLEMAN, Warner
Listed in Turloch, Tryon County, New York Militia 1775-77 and later in Butler's Rangers.
Source - SJJB

CASLEMAN, William
Listed in Turloch, Tryon County, New York Militia 1775-77 and later in Butler's Rangers.
Source - SJJB

CHACE (CHASE), Ammi
From Sandwich, Barnstable County, Massachusetts (Cape Cod). Was a gentleman. Says he was banished and left in 1777. He was found to be part of a Tory underground.
Source - LMTOS & SA

CHACE (CHASE), Levi
From Sandwich, Barnstable County, Massachusetts (Cape Cod). Was banished and jailed in 1777.
Source - DH

CHACE (CHASE), Levi Jr.
Was labeled as a loyalist, but he stayed.
Source - SA

CHALMERS, James Lieut. Col.
Listed on 11 July 1778 Muster Roll, First Battalion of Maryland Loyalist at Long Island, New York. He enlisted 14 Oct. 1777.
Source - ML

CHAMBERS, Elijah
Listed in New Jersey Volunteers muster roll commanded under Col. Joseph Barton and Capt. James Shaw dated 1 March 1777.
Source - NJM

CHAMBERS, Nathaniel
Listed as Private on muster roll of Major Thomas Barclay's company in the Loyal American Regiment commanded by Col. Beverly Robinson at Guanus on 11 May 1782.
Source - DSR2

CHATTERLON, Jacob
Listed as Private on muster roll of Capt. John Howard's company of New York Volunteers commanded by Lieut. Col. George Turnbull Esq., Commandant at Paulus Hook, February 1778.
Source - DSR3

CHERRY, Joseph
Listed as Private on muster roll of Capt. John Howard's company of New York Volunteers commanded by Lieut. Col. George Turnbull Esq., Commandant at Paulus Hook, February 1778.
Source - DSR3

CHEVER, George
Late of Sussex County, New Jersey, listed in inquisition 9 Feb. 1779 at Sussex Court of Inquiry by Isaac Martin and Samuel Meeker, Commissioners.
Source - NJNE

CHILDERHOUSE (?), John
Listed as a Private on May 1783 Muster Roll of Lieut. Col. Stephen Delancey, commanded by Col. Cortland Skinner Esq. at New Town (location unclear).
Source - DMR

CHOSEL, Jonathan
Late of Sussex County, New Jersey listed in inquisition 9 Feb. 1779 at Sussex Court of Inquiry by Isaac Martin and Samuel Meeker, Commissioners.
Source - NJNE

CHRISTIE, John
Listed as loyalist settler in Cornwall, Ontario in 1790's with 5 dependants, two girls at LaChine.
Source - LCO

CHUNK, Peter
Listed with Sir John Johnston's Brigade and later joined Joseph Brant's Volunteers. Disbanded in 1783 and possibly granted land in Niagara, Ontario.
Source - SJJB

CHURCH, William
Granted 500 acres in Rawdon/Douglas, Nova Scotia under Major General Small.
Source - WWRD

CLANDENING, John
Listed on New Jersey Volunteers muster roll commanded under Col. Joseph Barton and Capt. James Shaw dated 30 Jan. 1777.
Source - NJM

CLARK, Alexander Adjutant
Granted with others 8,900 acres 15 Oct. 1784 by Gov. Parr in Kings County, Nova Scotia.
Source - HKC#2

CLARK, Francis Sergeant
From Turloch, Tryon Co., New York. Served in Turloch Militia under Capt. Jacob Miller from 1775-77, then transferred to First Battalion of Kings Royal Rangers of New York. Possibly settled around Williamsburg, Ontario.
Source - SJJB

CLARKE, John
Listed as Private on muster roll of Capt. Jonathan Randall's company in His Majesty's Loyal American Regiment commanded by Col. Beverly Robinson on 27 August 1778, listed as prisoner with Rebels (location unknown).
Source - DSR2

CLARKE, Thomas
Listed as Private on muster roll of Capt. Jonathan Randall's company in His Majesty's Loyal American Regiment commanded by Col. Beverly Robinson on 27 August 1778 (location unknown), noted; Comm at Loyds Neck.
Source - DSR2

CLAUBACK, Henry
Listed as a Private and prisoner with the Rebels on Muster Roll of Capt. Peter Rutton's Company in the 4th. Battalion of New Jersey Volunteers commanded by Lieut. Col. Abraham Buskirk at Powles Hook 7 July 1779.
Source - DSR

CLEGHORN (Clighorn), Robert (Robart)
Listed as a Private on Muster Roll of Capt. Peter Ruton's Company in the 4th. Battalion of New Jersey Volunteers commanded by Lieut. Col. Abraham Buskirk at Staten Island, New York possibly in August or September and October and 30 Dec. 1778. He enlisted on 27 July 1778. Also listed on Jan. 1779 (location unknown) as with Southern Army. On March 1779 Muster at Hobuck (Hoboken), New Jersey and at Powles Hook 7 July 1779. On possible August 1779 Muster (place unknown) and at Governor's Island on 29 Oct. 1779 and Dec. 1779 stating he was "On ye Detachment". Also on 19 March 1780 muster (location unknown) and listed as "On Expedition with The Commander in Chief" and again in May 1780 with General Clinton. On 14 July and 11 Sept. and 2 Dec. 1780 muster at Staten Island, New York listed as "On Southern Expedition". Listed on 29 April 1781 muster at Staten Island, but deserted with the Southern Army.
Source - DSR

CLOUD, Rebecca
Granted with other refugee loyalist's 21, 380 acres by Gov. Parr 8 Aug. 1795 (85?) in Kings County, Nova Scotia.
Source - HKC#3

COBB, Anna (Perry)
Anna Perry married Nicolas Cobb in 1764 who were banished later as being loyalist in Sandwich, Massachusetts (Cape Cod).
Source - SA

COBB, Nicholas
From Sandwich, Barnstable County, Massachusetts (Cape Cod). Was a laborer and was banished from the state with family. Says he married Anna Perry in 1764. Was in the Tory underground and met at Seth Perry's house (see his listing) with other loyalists. He married Malatia Bourne and returned to Sandwich and became Town Clerk.
Source - DH & SA

COBB, Stephen
Labeled a loyalist and left per Betsey Keene, but mentioned in the Percival Diray that he was living at Snake Pond, Sandwich, Massachusetts (Cape Cod) in 1777.
Source - SA

COBURN, William
Listed in 4th. Battalion New Jersey Volunteers muster roll commanded by Lt. Col. Abraham Bushkirk and Capt. Peter Ruton (Ruttan)at Staten Island, New York dated March 1778. Listed as Private and died 1 March 1778. Again listed on 6 Jan. 1778 at same place as a Drummer, but sick in General Hospital. Again in March 1778 muster at same place and listed as dead on 1 March 1778.
Source - 4BNJVM & DSR

COCHRAN, John Capt. (Esq.)
Commander of Fort William and Henry in Portsmouth Harbor, New Hampshire and left on 24 Aug. 1775 on the ship, Canso with Gov. John Wentworth. Possibly traveled with him to Boston until March 1776 to Halifax, then too Philadelphia and on to London (not sure of this). Was listed at Flatbush, Long Island, New York with Gov. Wentworth around 1777. New Hampshire General Assembly listed him as the enemy along with 75 others in Nov. 1778. On confiscation list of 28 Nov. 1778. Settled in Saint John, New Brunswick and became a well-known gentleman.
Source - NHL

COCHRANE, John
On listed of loyalists granted land but info. not listed, but found in Rawdon/Douglas, Nova Scotia under Major General Small.
Source - WWRD

COLE, Daniel
Late of Sussex County, New Jersey, listed in inquisition 9 Feb. 1779 at Sussex Court of Inquiry by Isaac Martin and Samuel Meeker, Commissioners.
Source - NJNE

COLE, Edward Col.
Granted with other refugee loyalist's 21, 380 acres by Gov. Parr 8 Aug. 1795 (85?) in Kings County, Nova Scotia.
Source - HKC#3

COLE, Jacob
Listed as Private in 4th. Battalion New Jersey Volunteers muster roll commanded by Lt. Col. Abraham Bushkirk and Capt. Peter Ruton (Ruttan) at Staten Island, New York dated March 1778. Listed as prisoner with rebels. Also listed on 18 Nov. 1777 Muster at same place as taken prisoner on 29 Dec. 1776. He enlisted on 7 Dec. 1776. Again on 6 Jan. 1778 Muster at same place. Again in March, May, July and possibly August or September and October 1778 Muster at same place and still prisoner.
Source - 4BNJVM & DSR

COLE, Nathan
Listed as Private and confined with the Rebels on muster roll of Major Thomas Barclay's company in the Loyal American Regiment commanded by Col. Beverly Robinson at Guanus on 11 May 1782.
Source - DSR2

COLLINS (Collien)(Collens), Timothy
Listed as a Private on Muster Roll of Capt. Peter Ruton's Company in the 4th. Battalion of New Jersey Volunteers commanded by Lieut. Col. Abraham Buskirk (Bushkirk) at Staten Island, New York in May and July and possibly August or September, October and 30 Dec. 1778 and again possibly in Jan. 1779. On March 1779 Muster at Hobuck (Hoboken), New Jersey and at Powles Hook 7 July 1779. On possible August 1779 Muster (place unknown) and at Governor's Island on 29 Oct. 1779 and Dec. 1779. Also on 19 March and May 1780 muster (location unknown). On 14 July and 11 Sept. and 2 Dec. (note that he is "on Board Sloop Neptune")1780 muster at Staten Island, New York. Listed on 29 April 1781 muster at Staten Island.
Source - DSR

COLWELL, John
From Turloch, Tryon Co., New York. Served in Turloch Militia under Capt. Jacob Miller from 1775-77, then transferred to First Battalion, Kings Royal Rangers of New York. Possibly settled around Williamsburgh, Ontario.
Source - SJJB

COMLY, Peter
Listed as Private who was noted as "Transferred in the vacant company" on muster roll of Capt. John Howard's company of New York Volunteers

commanded by Lieut Col. George Turnbull Esq., Commandant at Paulus Hook, February 1778.
Source - DSR3

CONDON, Philip Corporal
Listed on muster roll of First Battalion of Maryland Loyalists 11 July 1778 at Long Island, New York. Enlisted 8 Dec. 1777.
Source - ML

CONKLIN, Samuel
Listed as a Private who enlisted 1 Oct. 1778 and on Muster Roll of Capt. Peter Ruton's Company of the 4th. Battalion of New Jersey Volunteers commanded by Lieut Col. Abraham Buskirk at Staten Island, New York in October 1778. Also listed at same place on Muster dated 30 Dec. 1778. On March 1779 Muster at Hobuck (Hoboken), New Jersey and at Powles Hook 7 July 1779 and again on August 1779 muster in same company and at Governor's Island on 29 Oct. 1779 and Dec. 1779. Also on 19 March and May 1780 muster (location unknown). On 14 July and 11 Sept. 1780 muster at Staten Island, New York.
Source - DSR

CONOLLY (Konnely), John
Listed as a Private on Muster Roll of Capt. Peter Ruton's Company in the 4th. Battalion of New Jersey Volunteers commanded by Lieut. Col. Abraham Bushkirk at Staten Island, New York in May and July and possibly August or September 1778. It says he was sick and in New York Hospital. October 1778 and Jan. 1779 Muster has him with Major Browne. On March 1779 Muster at Hobuck (Hoboken), New Jersey and sick in New York and later at Powles Hook 7 July 1779 still sick in New York and on August 1779 muster, still sick in New York and at Governor's Island on 29 Oct. and Dec. (Sick in New York)1779 with Major Brown. Also on 19 March and May 1780 muster (location unknown), but still with Major Browne. On 14 July and 11 Sept. and 2 Dec. 1780 muster at Staten Island, New York. Listed on 29 April 1781 muster at Staten Island still with Major Brown in New York.
Source - DSR

CONTRACK, Solomon
Late of Sussex County, New Jersey, listed in inquisition 9 Feb. 1779 at Sussex Court of Inquiry by Isaac Martin and Samuel Meeker, Commissioners.
Source - NJNE

COOK, Seth
Listed with Sir John Johnston's Brigade and later joined Joseph Brant's Volunteers. Disbanded in 1783 and possibly granted land in Niagara, Ontario.
Source - SJJB

COONUT, Roger
Listed on land grant petition with others to John Graves Simcoe, Esq. 12 July 1793 for land located between Long Point and Turkey Point on the west side of Lake Erie.
Source - EGRS

COOPER, Thomas
Listed as loyalist settler in Cornwall, Ontario in 1790's and was old and infirm, not able to work.
Source - LCO

COPE (Coope), George
Listed as a Private on Muster Roll in Capt. Peter Ruton's Company in the 4th. Battalion of New Jersey Volunteers commanded by Lieut. Col. Abraham Buskirk (Bushkirk) at Staten Island, New York in July 1778. It says that he was with Capt. Hatden at New York, and again in October and 30 Dec. Muster and possibly Jan. 1779 (place not given). On March 1779 Muster at Hobuck (Hoboken), New Jersey and at Powles Hook 7 July 1779 and again on August 1779 muster in same company and at Governor's Island on 29 Oct. 1779 and Dec. 1779. Also on 19 March and May 1780 muster (location unknown). On 14 July and 11 Sept. and 2 Dec. 1780 muster at Staten Island, New York. Listed on 29 April 1781 muster at Staten Island.
Source - DSR

COPE, Stephen
Listed as a Private on Muster Roll of Capt. Peter Ruton's Company in the 4th. Battalion of New Jersey Volunteers commanded by Lieut. Col. Abraham Bushkirk at Staten Island, New York in May 1778 and possibly August or September 1778 Muster with Capt. Hayden.
Source - DSR

COTTON, Roland
Born 13 Nov. 1701 in Sandwich, Barnstable County, Massachusetts (Cape Cod). Died 16 May 1778 at Sandwich. Member of either General Assembly or Council. Educated at Harvard in 1719. Was a colonel and

justice of the peace. His brother was Josiah Cotton. Was married to Deborah Mason on 30 Oct. 1760. She died August 1766. His mother was Elizabeth Saltonstall.
Source - DH

CORNRAD (Counrate), Nicholas (Nicholass)
Listed as a Private in 4th. Battalion New Jersey Volunteers muster roll commanded by Lt. Col. Abraham Bushkirk and Capt. Peter Ruton at Staten Island, New York dated March 1778. Listed as Private and died 20 Jan. 1778. Also listed on 18 Nov. 1777 Staten Island, New York Muster stating he inlisted on 7 Dec. 1776. Again on 6 Jan. 1778 Muster in same place. Again in March 1778 Muster at same place and as dead on 20 Jan. 1778.
Source - 4BNJVM & DSR

CORTLAND, Philip
Listed as an Ensign on Long Island, New York on Muster Roll of Capt. Peter Ruton's Company in the 4th. Battalion of New Jersey Volunteers commanded by Lieut. Col. Abraham Buskirk possibly in August 1779 (place unknown).
Source - DSR

COULTER, John
Granted 500 acres at Five-Mile River, Nova Scotia under Major General Small.
Source - WWRD

COULTER, William
Granted 500 acres at Five-Mile River, Nova Scotia under Major General Small.
Source - WWRD

COX, John
From Falmouth, Maine or Massachusetts? Left in 1783 to Cornwallis, Nova Scotia.
Source - DH

COX, Thomas
Listed as Private on muster roll of Capt. William Gray's company of New York Volunteers from 24 Feb. to 24 April 1781, location unknown.
Source - DSR3

CRAIN (Crane), Daniel
Listed as Corporal on muster roll of Capt. John Howard's company of New York Volunteers commanded by Lieut. Col. George Turnbull Esq., Commandant at Paulus Hook, February 1778. Also on muster of Capt. William Gray (same company) from 24 Feb. to 24 April 1781, as on command.
Source - DSR3

CRANNELL, Robert
Listed as Corporal on muster roll of Capt. John Howard's company of New York Volunteers commanded by Lieut. Col. George Turbull Esq., Commandant at Paulus Hook, February 1778.
Source - DSR3

CRAWFOOT, David
Listed with Sir John Johnston's Brigade and later joined Joseph Brant's Volunteers. Disbanded in 1783 and possibly granted land in Niagara, Ontario.
Source - SJJB

CRAWFORD, William
Listed as a Private on Muster Roll of Capt. Peter Ruttan's Company in the 4th. Battalion of New Jersey Volunteers commanded by Lieut. Col. Abraham Buskirk Esq. (location not given) in possibly Jan. 1779 as in the Regiment Hospital. Listed again on 2 Dec. 1780 muster at Staten Island, New York. On 29 April 1781 muster at Staten Island, enlisted by Capt. Buskirk. His was foot bitten and was sent off.
Source - DSR

CREDERMAN, (widow)
Listed as widow of loyalist, settled in Cornwall, Ontario in 1790's with 5 dependants, girls on the farm.
Source - LCO

CRELLEY, August
Listed on muster roll of First Battalion of Maryland Loyalists 11 July 1778 at Long Island, New York. Enlisted Dec. 1777.
Source - ML

CRISTY, William
Late of Sussex County, New Jersey, listed in inquisition 9 Feb. 1779 at Sussex Court of Inquiry by Isaac Martin and Samuel Meeker, Commissioners.
Source - NJNE

CRIZETT, Benjamin
Listed on muster roll of First Battalion of Maryland Loyalists 11 July 1778 at Long Island, New York. Enlisted 26 Nov. 1777.
Source - ML

CROCKER, Mr. (Old Man)
Jailed in Barnstable, Massachusetts (Cape Cod) goal with Otis Loring, Seth Perry (see his listing for more information) and a Mr. Davis and others for being loyalists. They later escaped to Newport, Rhode Island, British territory.
Source - SA

CROCKER, Josiah
Born 30 Dec. 1744. Died 4 May 1780 in Barnstable, Massachusetts (Cape Cod). Educated at Harvard in 1765 and became a schoolteacher and town clerk. He married 6 Oct. 1765 to Deborah Davis, daughter of Daniel Davis. Sons were, Uriel, Robert and Josiah. Daughters were, Deborah and Mehitable. His father was Cornelius Crocker and mother was Lydia Jenkins. They remained in state after British left.
Source - DH

CRON, John
Listed in New Jersey Volunteers muster roll commanded under Col. Joseph Barton and Capt. James Shaw dated 1 March 1777.
Source - NJM

CRONCK, James
Listed as Private on muster roll of Capt. Jonathan Randall's company in His Majesty's Loyal American Regiment commanded by Col. Beverly Robinson on 27 Aug. 1778 (location unknown).
Source - DSR2

CROUSE, John
Listed in First Batalion of Kings Royal Rangers of New York as a Private 1775-77. From Turloch, Tryon County, New York. Possibly settled at Williamburg, Ontario after 1783.
Source - SJJB

CRYSELOR, Filip
Listed as Private in First Battalion of Kings Royal Rangers of New York 1775-77. From Turloch, Tryon County, New York. Possibly settled at Williamsburg, Ontario after 1783.
Source SJJB

CRYSELOR, John
Listed in First Battalion of Kings Royal Rangers of New York as a Private 1775-77. From Turloch, Tryon County, New York. Possibly settled at Williamsburg, Ontario after 1783.
Source - SJJB

CROWELL, Joseph
Late of Sussex County, New Jersey in inquisition 9 Feb. 1779 at Court of Inquiry at Sussex by Isaac Martin and Samuel Meeker, Commissioners.
Source - NJNE

CUMMING, William
Listed as loyalist settler in Cornwall, Ontario in 1790's alone.
Source - LCO

CUMMINGS, Samuel Esq.
From Hollis, NH. The New Hampshire General Assembly listed him and 75 others as the enemy in Nov. 1778.
Source - NHL

CUMMINGS, Thomas
A yeoman from Hollis, NH. The New Hampshire General Assembly listed him and 75 others as the enemy in Nov. 1778. On petition to change Conway to Digby, Nova Scotia 20 Feb. 1784.
Source - NHL

CUMMINGS, Thomas
From Falmouth, Maine?
Source - DH

CUMMINS, John
Listed on New Jersey Volunteers muster roll commanded by Col. Joseph Barton and Capt. James Shaw dated 26 Jan. 1777.
Source - NJM

CURTIS, John
Listed with Sir John Johnston's Brigade and later joined Joseph Brant's Volunteers. Disbanded in 1783 and possibly granted land in Niagara, Ontario.
Source - SJJB

CURTIS, Samuel
Late of Sussex County, New Jersey, listed in inquisition 9 Feb. 1779 at Sussex Court of Inquiry by Isaac Martin and Samuel Meeker, Commissioners.
Source - NJNE

CURTIS, Samuel
Listed as a Private on Muster Roll of Capt. Peter Ruton's Company in the 4th. Battalion of New Jersey Volunteers commanded by Lieut. Col. Abraham Buskirk (Bushkirk) at Staten Island, New York in May 1778 and who was deceased in April and July (as dead) 1778. (not sure if same person as above).
Source - DSR

CUTLER, Thomas
A gentleman from Keene, NH. The New Hampshire General Assembly listed him and 75 others as the enemy in Nov. 1778.
Source - NHL

CUTLER, Zaccheus
A trader from Amherst, NH. The New Hampshire General Assembly listed him and 75 others as the enemy in Nov. 1778. On confiscation list of 28 Nov. 1778.
Source - NHL

DALRYMPLE, James
Granted 500 acres at Douglas, Nova Scotia for serving in the 8th. Regiment. Also listed as getting 400 acres in Rawdon/Douglas, Nova Scotia under Major General Small. Listed again for 350 acres.
Source - WWRD

DARBY, Joseph
Listed as a Private on muster roll of Capt. Christopher Hatch's Company of Loyal Americans, commanded by Col. Beverly Robinson at Haarlem, New York, possibly at beginning of 1778 and on 21 April 1778 muster.
Source - DSR2

DAVIDSON, John
A yeoman from Londonderry, NH. The New Hampshire General Assembly listed him and 75 others as the enemy in Nov. 1778. Became a Lieut. and settled in New Brunswick, Canada and served as Deputy Surveyor of the province for years. He settled in Dumfries, York County and became a member of the House of Assembly in 1802.
Source - NHL

DAVIS, Mr.
Jail in Barnstable, Massachusetts (Cape Cod) goal with Otis Loring, Seth Perry (see his listing for more information) and old man Mr. Crocker and other loyalists. They later escaped to Newport, Rhode Island, British territory.
Source - SA

DAVIS, James
Listed as Private on muster roll of Capt. John Howard's company of New York Volunteers commanded by Lieut. Col. George Turnbull Esq., Commandant at Paulus Hook, February 1778.
Source - DSR3

DAVIS, Solomon
From Barnstable, Massachusetts (Cape Cod). Arrested 1776, but remained after British left.
Source - DH

DEDRICK, Lewis
Listed on land grant petition to John Graves Simcoe, Esq. 12 July 1793 for land located between Long Point and Turkey Point on the west side of Lake Erie.
Source - EGRS

DEGROOT (Degroat)(Degrot)(Degrote), David (Davod)
Listed in 4th. Battalion New Jersey Volunteers muster roll commanded by Lt. Col. Abraham Bushkirk and Capt. Peter Ruton (Ruttan) at Staten Island, New York dated March 1778. Listed as Private and on Furlow.

Also listed on 18 Nov. 1777 at Staten Island, New York as on command recruiting and who inlisted on 7 Dec. 1776. Again on 6 Jan. 1778 Muster at same place and recruiting others. Again in March, May, July and possibly August or September 1778 Muster at same place and on Furlow May July. Also listed in possible October and 30 Dec. (as sick) 1778 Muster and on Jan. 1779 (location unknown) as a prisoner with the Rebels. On March 1779 Muster at Hobuck (Hoboken), New Jersey and at Powles Hook 7 July 1779. On possible August 1779 Muster (place unknown) and at Governor's Island on 29 Oct. 1779 and Dec. 1779. Also on 19 March and May 1780 muster (location unknown). On 14 July and 11 Sept. and 2 Dec. 1780 muster at Staten Island, New York. Listed on 29 April 1781 muster at Staten Island.
Source - 4BNJVM & DSR

DEIGHTON, John Sargent
Listed on muster roll of First Battalion of Maryland Loyalists 11 July 1778 at Long Island, New York. Enlisted 4 Dec. 1777. Taken prisoner 18 June 1778.
Source - ML

DELANCEY, Oliver
Lived at New York, but listed in Sussex County, New Jersey in inquisition of 9 Feb. 1779, court of inquiry by Isaac Martin and Samuel Meeker, Commissioners.
Source NJNE

DELANCEY, Stephen
Listed as Lieut. Colonel in Muster Roll May 1783 and later went to Nova Scotia.
Source - DMR

DELONG, Aaron
Listed as Private on muster roll of Major Thomas Barclay's company in the Loyal American Regiment commanded by Col. Beverly Robinson at Guanus on 11 May 1782.
Source - DSR2

DELONG, John
Listed as Private on muster roll of Major Thomas Barclay's company in the Loyal American Regiment commanded by Col. Beverly Robinson at Guanus on 11 May 1782.
Source - DSR2

DELONG, Simon
Listed as Private and Major Barclay's Agent on muster roll of Major Thomas Barclay's company in the Loyal American Regiment commanded by Col. Beverly Robinson at Guanus on 11 May 1782.
Source - DSR2

DEMERAY, Samuel
Listed as a Private on Muster Rolls of Capt. Peter Ruttan's Company in the 4th. Battalion of New Jersey Volunteers commanded by Lieut. Col. Abraham Buskirk Esq. (location not given) in possibly Jan. 1779. (Could this be Samuel Demorest listed below).
Source - DSR

DEMOREST (Demerist)(Demarest), Samuel
Listed in 4th. Battalion New Jersey Volunteers muster roll commanded by Lt. Col. Abraham Bushkirk and Capt. Peter Ruton (Ruttan) at Staten Island, New York dated March and May 1778. Listed as Private and prisoner with rebels. Also listed on 18 Nov. 1777 Muster at same place as taken prisoner on 29 Dec. 1776. He enlisted on 7 Dec. 1776. Again on 6 Jan. 1778 Muster at same place and still listed as prisoner. Again in March and July and possibly August or September 1778 Muster at same place and still prisoner. The October 1778 Muster says he enlisted 6 Dec. 1776 and was taken prisoner on 20 Dec. 1776 and returned on 2 Oct. 1778 with note saying, Not subsisted nor received bounty. Listed again at same place 30 Dec. 1778 Muster Roll. On March 1779 Muster at Hobuck (Hoboken), New Jersey and at Powles Hook 7 July 1779. On possible August 1779 Muster (place unknown) and at Governor's Island on 29 Oct. 1779 and on Dec. 1779 muster stating the he "Has not drawn his bounty". Also on 19 March and May 1780 muster (location unknown). On 14 July and 11 Sept. and 2 Dec. 1780 muster at Staten Island, New York. Listed on 29 April 1781 muster at Staten Island.
Source - 4BNJVM & DSR

DENNISON, Michael
Member of John Campbell's Grenadiers, volunteers from Ireland, First of Delaney's Brigade. He was also a Farmer. Died 15 April 1840, Penniac, York Co., New Brunswick, Canada. Wife's name unknown. Children: James, b.13 Sept. 1789, d. after 1861. Married Abigail Manzer, Margaret, Catherine, Mary, Sarah, Susannah, Grace and Bridget. Michael's will was filed 29 July 1840, York Co., New Brunswick, Canada.
Source - AGD

DEVALL, Edward
Listed as Private on muster roll of Capt. John Howard's company of New York Volunteers commanded by Lieut. Col. George Turnbull Esq., Commandant at Paulus Hook, February 1778.
Source - DSR3

DEVOE, Daniel
Listed as Corporal on Comm. at Loyds Neck on Capt. Jonathan Randall's company muster roll in His Majesty's Loyal American Regiment commanded by Col. Beverly Robinson on 27 August 1778 (muster location unknown).
Source - DSR2

DEVONPORT, Joseph
Listed on muster roll of First Battalion of Maryland Loyalists 11 July 1778 at Long Island, New York. Enlisted 6 Nov. 1777.
Source - ML

DEWEL, Wilber
Listed as Private, absent with leave on muster roll of Capt. William Gray's company of New York Volunteers from 24 Feb. to 24 April 1781, location unknown.
Source - DSR3

DIAMOND, Peter
Listed as Private on muster roll of Capt. John Howard's company of New York Volunteers commanded by Lieut. Col. George Turnbull Esq., Commandant at Paulus Hook, February 1778. Also listed on muster as being in General Hospital, of Capt. William Gray (same company) from 24 Feb. to 24 April 1781, location unknown.
Source - DSR3

DICKEY, John Corporal
Listed on muster roll of First Battalion of Maryland Loyalists 11 July 1778 at Long Island, New York. Enlisted 6 Nov. 1777.
Source - ML

DIX, Jonathan
A trader from Pembroke, NH. New Hampshire General Assembly listed him and 75 others as the enemy in Nov. 1778.
Source - NHL

DONIVIL, James
Listed on muster roll of First Battalion of Maryland Loyalists 11 July 1778 at Long Island, New York. Enlisted 1 Nov. 1777.
Source - ML

DOPP, David
Listed as Corporal on muster roll of Major Thomas Barclay's company in the Loyal American Regiment commanded by Col. Beverly Robinson at Guanus on 11 May 1782 with note saying he was in the General Hospital, but another notation says he died 6 June 1782.
Source - DSR2

DOUGAN, Henry Surgeon(?)
Listed in Gen. Skinner's Brigade muster roll, Seconded Officers (date unknown) at age 46 (or 26) from Ireland.
Source - GSB

DUFFINS(?), Edward
Listed as a Private on May 1783 Muster Roll of Lieut. Col. Stephen Delancey, commanded by Col. Cortland Skinner Esq. at New Town (location unclear).
Source - DMR

DULANY, Grafton Capt.
Listed on muster roll of First Battalion of Maryland Loyalists, 11 July 1778 at Long Island, New York. Enlisted Nov. 1777.
Source - ML

DULYEE, Peter
Listed as Private in 4th. Battalion New Jersey Volunteers muster roll commanded by Lt. Col. Abraham Bushkirk and Capt. Peter Ruton at Staten Island, New York dated March 1778. Listed as discharged.
Source - 4BNJVM & DSR

DUNHAM, Asher Lieut.
Granted with other loyalist refugee's 21,380 acres by Gov. Parr 8 Aug. 1795(85?) in Kings County, Nova Scotia. Also listed in Gen. Skinner's Brigade muster roll, Seconded Officers (date unknown) at age 38 from America.
Source - HKC#3 & GSB

DUMAINE, William
Granted with other refugee loyalist's 21, 380 acres by Gov. Parr 8 Aug. 1795 (85?) in Kings County, Nova Scotia.
Source - HKC#3

DUSENBURY, Benjamin
Listed as Private on muster roll of Capt. John Howard's company of New York Volunteers commanded by Lieut. Col. George Turnbull Esq., Commandant at Paulus Hook, February 1778.
Source - DSR3

DUSENBURY, Stephen
Listed as Sergeant on muster roll of Capt. John Howard's company of New York Volunteers commanded by Lieut. Col. George Turnbull Esq., Commandant at Paulus Hook, February 1778.
Source - DSR3

DUTTON, ...? Private
Granted land in Douglas, Nova Scotia on 13 Dec. 1785 for serving in the 2nd. Battalion, 84th. Regiment.
Source - WWRD

ELDRIDGE, Joshua
From Falmouth, Maine or Massachusetts? Was a mariner and was banished and left the state.
Source - DH

ELLIS/ELLES, Abiel (Abel)
From Sandwich, Barnstable County, Massachusetts (Cape Cod). Cited by town or committee of correspondence for being a Tory. He was jailed in 1778, but remained after British left. He was placed in jail for not taking the oath, but is said to have stayed.
Source - DH & SA

ELLIS, Christopher
Son of Elnathan Ellis, who was the son of Manoah who was the son of John Ellis. He was born 10 March 1717/18 in Yarmouth, Barnstable County, (Cape Cod) Massachusetts. His mother was Mary Burgess. Living in Sandwich, Massachusetts he married 12 Oct. 1739 to Priscilla Chase, daughter of Thomas Chase and Sarah Gowell of Dennis, Barnstable County, Massachusetts. She was born 10 April 1720 in Yarmouth, Mass.. They had the following children, all born in Yarmouth, Mass.: Levi, b.

1739, Ebenezer, b. 1742, Lazarus, b. 1744. Christopher possibly relocated to Hardyston, Sussex Co., New Jersey before Jan. 1774. He and family were also recorded around Warwick, Orange Co., New York 1773-74. This family was supporters of the British and was considered Loyalists.
Source - EGRS

ELLIS, Ebenezer
Son of Christopher Ellis and Mary Burgess of Yarmouth, Barnstable Co. (Cape Cod), Massachusetts. Born 25 July 1742 at that same place. Was considered a loyalist. Resettled at Warwick, Orange Co., New York 1773-4. Also shows up in Hardyston, Sussex Co., New Jersey Sept. 1774, May 1780 and Jan. 1781 on tax lists. He sided with the British. He moved to Wyoming Valley, Luzerne Co., Pennsylvania 1 Feb. 1787 and at Chemung Town, Montgomery Co., New York (now Tioga Co.) in 1790 (Fed. Census). Found on a 12 July 1793 land petition in Canada dated 12 July 1793 with son Cornwall. Returned to Barton, Tioga Co., NY just before 1800. Died after 1810 and was buried in what later became a gravel pit on the property of John Hanna in that same town. Married Betsey ......? who was born before 1756 and she died after 1800 and is buried with Ebenezer at same location. Children were: Ebenezer Jr. b. 1765, Samual b. 1770, Cornwall (Conway) b.c. 1776, Jesse b. before 1784, William b. 1787, Abigail and possibly 7 other children. Inquisition against him and others on 10 March 1779, Sussex Co., New Jersey, published in NJ Gazette at Trenton, NJ. He was also put into jail for a time.
Source - EGRS

ELLIS, Ebenezer
Son of Ephraim and Mary Ellis Jr. of Sandwich, Barnstable County, Massachusetts (Cape Cod) who's mother petitioned 17 June 1778 the Massachusetts House of Representative to let her join her husband in exile which was granted 14 Dec. 1778.
Source - SA

ELLIS, Ephraim
From Sandwich, Barnstable County, Massachusetts (Cape Cod). Was a Yeoman. Cited by town or committee of correspondence for being a Tory in 1778. His Barnstable property was forfeited in 1780. He was banished and left the state. Wife was named Mary who visited from Long Island, New York during their stay there as loyalist refugees. Wanting to return to the Patriot side, he died in 1783 never to enjoy liberty. His wife married Thomas Nye.
Source - DH & SA

ELLIS, Ephraim Jr.
(Not sure if the above Ephraim is this Junior?) Was in the Tory underground in Sandwich, Barnstable County, Massachusetts (Cape Cod) and met at Seth Perry's house (see his listing) with other loyalists and was banished. Children were: Ephraim and Ebenezer.
Source - SA

ELLIS, Ephraim
Son of Ephraim and Mary Ellis Jr. of Sandwich, Barnstable County, Massachusetts (Cape Cod) who was listed on mothers petition 17 June 1778 to the Massachusetts House of Representetives to let her join her husband which was granted 14 Dec. 1778.
Source - SA

ELLIS, Lazarus
Son of Christopher Ellis and Mary Burgess of Yarmouth, Barnstable Co., (Cape Cod), Massachusetts. Born 1 Sept. 1744 at that same place. Was considered a loyalist. Resettled and is listed on Hardyston, Sussex Co., New Jersey tax lists for Sept. 1774, May 1780, Aug. 1780 and Jan. 1781. Shows up near Warwick, Orange Co., New York 1773-4 and at Tunkhannock, Wyoming Co., Pennsylvania 1796 and again in Wyalusing District, Bradford Co., Pa. between 18 Feb. 1807 and 3 July 1807 and in Braintrim, Luzerne Co., Pa.. Married Sarah ......? Children were: Thomas and Mary and possibly others. Will was dated 18 Feb. 1807 at Luzerne Co., Pa.. Died before 21 Aug. 1807 at Braintrim, Pa..
Source - EGRS

ELLIS, Levi
Son of Christopher Ellis and Mary Burgess of Yarmouth, Barnstable Co., (Cape Cod) Massachusetts. Born 6 March 1739 at that same place. Questionable if he was a loyalist. Relocated to Vernon, Sussex Co., New York c. 1770-98, then to Ovid, Seneca Co., NY. Listed on Hardyston, Sussex Co., New Jersey Sept. 1774 tax list. Was possibly a Baptist while living near or in Warwick, Orange Co., NY 1775. Operated a grist mill, farm and blacksmith business. He was possibly a widower after 1775. He died 1815. Second marriage between 1776 and 1790 to Elizabeth ....? 1776 or 1790. Children were: Elizabeth b.c. 1760, William b. 1762, Levi Jr. b. 1764, Lazarus b. 1766, Abner, Amos, Archibald, Barbara, Nancy, Simeon b.c. 1775. Second marriage children were: Anna b. 1785-90, d. 1817, Will and probate record of 3 July 1815, Ovid, Seneca Co., NY, Moses b. 1792, Charlotte b. 1795-1800. d. 1817 NY. Was listed in Fourth Battalion of New Jersey Volunteers 25 March 1777. Property was sold off

on 9 April 1777 and again on 18 July 1777. Inquisition against him and others in Sussex Co., New Jersey 10 March 1779, published in NJ Gazette at Trenton, NJ. (Record does not show him fleeing to Canada or other loyalists resettlement areas).
Source - EGRS

ELLIS, Mary (Perry)
Wife of Ephraim Ellis Jr., who were labeled as loyalist. She was allowed to visit family in Sandwich, Massachusetts (Cape Cod) while they were loyalists refugee's living on Long Island, New York. Their estate was confiscated. She petitioned the Massachusetts House of Representetives 17 June 1778 to let her join her husband in exile which was granted 14 Dec. 1778. Children were Ephraim and Ebenezer. After the death in 1783 of Ephraim, she married Thomas Nye and probably returned to Sandwich.
Source - SA

ELLIS, Neisor
Listed on land grant petition with others 12 July 1793 to John Graves Simcoe, Esq. for land located between Long Point and Turkey Point on the west side of Lake Erie. (could this be a nickname for Ebenezer?)
Source - EGRS

ELLIS, Thomas
Relation to Christopher Ellis and Mary Burgess of Yarmouth, Barnstable Co., (Cape Cod), Massachusetts. He was born between 1766 and 1775 possibly at the above listed location. Considered a loyalist and listed with Levi and Ebenezer Ellis as such in Sussex Co., New Jersey in 1779. His property was auctioned off on 27 May 1777. Shows up in Hardyston, Sussex Co., NJ tax lists of May and Aug.1780 and Jan. 1781. Appears in the 1810, 1820 Federal Census and the 1825 New York Census at Ellistown, Tioga Co., NY. He appears in publication of Pioneer and Patriot Families of Bradford County, Pennsylvania 1770-1800, which I question his loyalist standing. On 29 Nov. 1777 he deserted from the Fourth Battalion of New Jersey Volunteers.

ELLISON, Robert
Listed in New Jersey Volunteers muster roll commanded under Col. Joseph Barton and Capt. James Shaw dated 26 Jan. 1777 (listed 3 times) and on 13 Dec. 1776.
Source - NJM

EMANUEL, Henry
Listed in 4th. Battalion New Jersey Volunteers muster roll commanded by Lt. Col. Abraham Bushkirk and Capt. Peter Ruton at Staten Island, New York dated March and May and possibly August or September 1778. Listed as Private and prisoner with rebels. Another Henry, same rank but discharged. October 1778 Muster also lists him as a prisoner.
Source - 4BNJVM & DSR

EMANUEL, Henry
Listed in Muster Roll of Capt. Peter Ruttan's Company in the 4th. Battalion of New Jersey Volunteers commanded by Lieut. Col. Abraham Bushkirk at Staten Island, New York in March and July 1778. (This entry is listed as two people, one discharged, the other a prisoner).
Source - DSR

EMER, Peter
Listed as loyalist settler in Cornwall, Ontario in 1790's with 3 dependants on his land.
Source - LCO

EMER, Philip
Listed as loyalist settler in Cornwall, Ontario in 1790's with 1 dependant on his land.
Source - LCO

ESTMAN, Nadab
Listed as loyalist settler in Cornwall, Ontario in 1790's on his land.
Source - LCO

ETTINGER, Lewis
Granted 500 acres in Douglas, Nova Scotia for serving with 84th. Regiment. Also listed as getting 1300 acres in Rawdon/Douglas, Nova Scotia under Major General Small.
Source - WWRD

EVERY, Isaac
Listed as Private on muster roll of Capt. John Howard's company of New York Volunteers commanded by Lieut. Col. George Turnbull Esq., Commandant at Paulus Hook, February 1778.
Source - DSR3

EVERY, Thomas
Listed as Private who deserted on 26 Aug. 1777 on muster roll of Capt. William Gray's company of New York Volunteers from 24 Feb. to 24 April 1781, location unknown.
Source - DSR3

FARLING, John
Listed as loyalist settler in Cornwall, Ontario in 1790's with 2 dependants.
Source - LCO

FARNSWORTH, Daniel
A yeoman from New Ipswich, NH. The New Hampshire General Assembly listed him and 75 others as the enemy in Nov. 1778. On confiscation list of 28 Nov. 1778.
Source - NHL

FATER(?), Balhes
Listed as Private on muster roll of Capt. William Gray's company of New York Volunteers from 24 Feb. to 24 April 1781, location unknown.
Source - DSR3

FENTON, Jacob
Born c. 1755. He was a Sergeant in the King's Carolina Rangers, possibly not married during the war, but married in Nova Scotia to a Catherine. He came to Country Harbour, Nova Scotia.
Source - VNB

FENTON, John Esq.
In June 1775 a group of armed men caught John, an expelled member of the House of Assembly at Gov. John Wentworth's house and was jailed at Exeter, New Hampshire for being a loyalist. He later escaped and fled to England. The New Hampshire General Assembly listed him and 75 others as the enemy in Nov. 1778.
Source - NHL

FERGUSON, Alexander
Granted 500 acres (another listing for 333 1/3 acres. Not sure if another Alex or same person) at Douglas, Nova Scotia for serving in 84th. Regiment.
Source - WWRD

FERGUSON, John
Granted 400 acres in Douglas, Nova Scotia for serving in 2nd. Battalion, 84th. Regiment.
Source - WWRD

FERREL, Cornelius
Listed on muster roll of First Battalion of Maryland Loyalists 11 July 1778 at Long Island, New York. Enlisted 6 Nov. 1777.
Source - ML

FINCH, John
Listed on land grant petition with others 12 July 1793 to John Graves Simcoe, Esq. for land located between Long Point and Turkey Point on the west side of Lake Erie.
Source - EGRS

FINNEY, Francis Ensign
Granted with others 8,900 acres 15 Oct. 1784 by Gov. Parr in Kings County, Nova Scotia.
Source - HKC#2

FINNY/(PHINNEY?), Francis
From Sandwich, Barnstable County, Massachusetts (Cape Cod). Was a laborer and was banished and left the state.
Source - DH & LMTOS

FINTEN, Elijah
Late of Sussex County, New Jersey, listed in inquisition 9 Feb. 1779 at Sussex Court of Inquiry, by Isaac Martin and Samuel Meeker, Commissioners.
Source - NJNE

FISH, ...
He was listed as one of the loyalist that took part in the Sandwich Liberty Pole incident quoted by Abraham Holmes of Rochester, Massachusetts (Cape Cod Magazine Oct. 1915). This account was in Sandwich, Massachusetts (Cape Cod).
Source - SA

FISHER, John Esq.
Listed as a naval officer at Portsmouth, New Hampshire and possible brother-in-law of Gov. John Wentworth and became like Benjamin

Thompson of Concord, a secretary in the Colonial Secretary's office in London. The New Hampshire General Assembly listed him and 75 others as the enemy in Nov. 1778.
Source - NHL

FISHER, John
Listed on muster roll of First Battalion of Maryland Loyalists 11 July 1778 at Long Island, New York. Enlisted 14 Dec. 1777.
Source - ML

FISHER, Lewis
Listed on Muster Roll of Capt. Peter Ruttan's Company in the 4th. Battalion of the New Jersey Volunteers commanded by Col. Abraham Bushkirk at Staten Island New York 18 Nov. 1777. He was taken prisoner on 29 Dec. 1776 and enlisted 7 Dec. 1776. (not sure if the below Lodiwick is the same person?). Again listed on 6 Jan. 1778 Muster at same place and still a prisoner. On possibly August 1779 Muster (place unknown) and on Dec. 1779 saying the he "Has not drawn his bounty, Furlow".
Source - DSR

FISHER, Lodiwick (Lewick or Lewis)(Lodewick)(Lewish)
Listed in 4th. Battalion New Jersey Volunteers muster roll commanded by Lt. Col. Abraham Bushkirk and Capt. Peter Ruton at Staten Island, New York dated March 1778. Listed as Private an prisoner by rebels. Again in March 1778 Muster at same place and still prisoner. The October 1778 Muster says he enlisted 6 Dec. 1776, taken prisoner 20 Dec. 1776 and returned on 2 Oct. 1778. Note says, Not subsisted nor received bounty. Again listed on 30 Dec. 1778 Muster at same place. Also Muster of Jan. 1779 (place unknown). On March 1779 Muster at Hobuck (Hoboken), New Jersey and at Powles Hook 7 July 1779 and at Governor's Island on 29 Oct. 1779. Also on 19 March and May 1780 muster (location unknown). On 14 July and 11 Sept. (sick in regiment hospital) and 2 Dec. 1780 muster (still in regiment hospital) at Staten Island, New York. Listed on 29 April 1781 muster at Staten Island.
Source - 4BNJVM & DSR

FISHER, Peter
Listed in 4th. Battalion New Jersey Volunteers muster roll commanded by Lt. Col. Abraham Bushkirk and Capt. Peter Ruton (Ruttan) at Staten Island, New York dated March 1778. Listed as Private and prisoner by rebels. Also listed on 18 Nov. 1777 Muster at same place as taken prisoner on 29 Dec. 1776. He enlisted 7 Dec. 1776. Again on 6 Jan. 1778

Muster at same place and still prisoner. Again in March 1778 Muster at same place and still prisoner and on Jan. 1779 Muster (location unknown) and at Powles Hook 7 July 1779, still a prisoner and again on August 1779 muster in same company and at Governor's Island on 29 Oct. and Dec. 1779 still prisoner. Also on 19 March and May 1780 muster (location unknown)(prisoner). On 14 July and 11 Sept. and 2 Dec. 1780 muster at Staten Island, New York (prisoner). Listed on 29 April 1781 muster at Staten Island (prisoner).
Source - 4BNJVM & DSR

FLANAGAN, Christopher
Listed as Private on muster roll of Capt. Christopher Hatch's Company of Loyal Americans, commanded by Col. Beverly Robinson at Haarlem, New York, possibly beginning of 1778. It is noted that he was dead 26 Oct. 1777 and listed again on 21 April 1778 as dead.
Source - DSR2

FLEAGLER, William
Listed as Sergeant, in command on muster roll of Capt. William Gray's company of New York Volunteers from 24 Feb. to 24 April 1781, location unknown.
Source - DSR3

FOLGER, Timothy
Lived formerly in Nantucket Island, Massachusetts (Cape Cod), then Dartmouth and then Nova Scotia in December 1790 with Samuel Starbuck. He had considerable property on Nantucket and owned five whaling vessels which all suffered damage in the cause of the King's war. At the end of the war Starbuck went to Nova Scotia and continued whaling. The British government was petitioned for help (Chatham papers p. 220).
Source - LMTMPC

FORBES, John
From Tryon County, New York near the Mohawk River. Was Sir John Johnson's Tenant. He was taken prisoner in April 1780.
Source - HP

FOSTER, Stephen
Listed as a Private on Muster Roll of Capt. Peter Ruton's Company in the 4th. Battalion of New Jersey Volunteers commanded by Lieut. Col. Abraham Bushkirk at Staten Island, New York in May, July and possibly

August or September, October and 30 Dec. 1778, possibly Jan. 1779 (place unknown) Muster. On March 1779 Muster at Hobuck (Hoboken), New Jersey and at Powles Hook 7 July 1779. On possible August 1779 Muster (place unknown) and at Governor's Island on 29 Oct. 1779 and Dec. 1779 as sick. Also on 19 March and May 1780 muster (location unknown). On 14 July and 11 Sept. and 2 Dec. 1780 muster at Staten Island, New York. Listed on 29 April 1781 muster at Staten Island.
Source - DSR

FOWLER, Elijah Lieut.
Granted with other loyalist refugee's 21,380 acres by Gov. Parr 8 Aug. 1795(85?) in Kings County, Nova Scotia.
Source - HKC#3

FOWLER, Francis
Listed as Private on muster roll of Capt. William Gray's company of New York Volunteers from 24 Feb. to 24 April 1781, location unknown.
Source - DSR3

FOWLER, Jeremiah
Listed as Sergeant on muster roll of Capt. Jonathan Randall's company in His Majesty's Loyal American Regiment commanded by Col. Beverly Robinson on 27 August 1778 (location unknown).
Source - DSR2

FOWLER (Fowle), Robert Lieut.
A printer from Exeter, NH. The New Hampshire General Assembly listed him and 75 others as the enemy in Nov. 1778. On confiscation list of 28 Nov. 1778.
Source - NHL

FOX, Fredrick
Listed as Private in First Battalion of Kings Royal Rangers of New York 1775-77. From Turloch, Tryon County, New York. Possibly settled at Williamsburg, Ontario after 1783.
Source - SJJB

FOX, George
Listed as a Private in 4th. Battalion New Jersey Volunteers muster roll commanded by Lt. Col. Abraham Bushkirk and Capt. Peter Ruton (Ruttan) at Staten Island, New York dated March 1778. Listed as Private and a Carpenter. Also listed on 18 Nov. 1777 Muster at same place stating

that he enlisted on 22 Jan. 1777. Again on 6 Jan. 1778 Muster at same place. Again in March 1778 Muster at same place and on command as Carpenter.
Source - 4BNJVM & DSR

FOX, James
Listed as Sergeant in 4th. Battalion New Jersey Volunteers muster roll commanded by Lt. Col. Abraham Bushkirk and Capt. Peter Ruton (Ruttan) at Staten Island, New York dated March 1778. Listed as Private and dead. Also listed on 18 Nov. 1777 Muster at same place where he was sick at the Regiment Hospital. He enlisted on 7 Dec. 1776. Again on 6 Jan. 1778 Muster at same place as sick in General Hospital. Again in March 1778 Muster at same place and as dead.
Source - 4BNJVM & DSR

FOX, William
Listed as a Private in 4th. Battalion New Jersey Volunteers muster roll commanded by Lt. Col. Abraham Bushkirk and Capt. Peter Ruton (Ruttan) at Staten Island, New York dated March 1778. Listed as Private and a Carpenter. Also listed on 18 Nov. 1777 Muster at same place which states that he enlisted on 22 Jan. 1777. Again on 6 Jan. 1778 Muster at same place and on C.M (Command?). Again in March and May, July and possibly August or September at Flag Staff 1778 Muster at same place and on command as Carpenter. The October and 30 Dec. 1778 Muster list him as a Carpenter with Capt. Robinson. On March 1779 Muster at Hobuck (Hoboken), New Jersey on Furlow on Staten Island, New York and listed again at Powles Hook 7 July 1779. Listed again on August 1779 muster in same company and at Governor's Island on 29 Oct. and Dec. (deserted) 1779.
Source - 4BNJVM & DSR

FRAIR(?), Peter
Listed as Private, confined with the rebels on muster roll of Major Thomas Barclay's company in the Loyal American Regiment commanded by Col. Beverly Robinson at Guanus on 11 May 1782.
Source - DSR2

FRAIRS, Nehemiah (see Travis?)

FRAIRS, Robert (see Travis?)

FRANEY, John
Listed as Sergeant on muster roll of Capt. John Howard's company of New York Volunteers commanded by Lieut. Col. George Turnbull Esq., Commandant at Paulus Hook, February 1778.
Source - DSR3

FRANEY, Thomas
Listed as Lieutenant on muster roll of Capt. John Howard's company of New York Volunteers commanded by Lieut. Col. George Turnbull Esq., Commandant at Paulus Hook, February 1778.
Source - DSR3

FRANKLIN, John Robinson
Granted 500 acres in Rawdon/Douglas, Nova Scotia under Major General Small.
Source - WWRD

FRASER, Donald (widow of)
The widow of Donald Fraser granted 250 acres in Douglas, Nova Scotia along with widow of Neil Fraser for serving in 2nd. Battalion, 84th. Regiment.
Source - WWRD

FRASER, Francis (Franas) Lieut.
Granted with others 8,900 acres in Kings County, Nova Scotia by Gov. Parr 15 Oct. 1784. He was born in New Jersey of Scottish lines. Married 26 Jan. 1769 to Dioderna Morris at Woodbridge, New Jersey by the Church of England. Joined the British in 1776 and winter of same year was taken prisoner in battle between New Brunswick and Amboy, New Jersey. Exchanged 29 Sept. 1778 for Lieut. Matthew Wideman of Col. Atlee's Continental Troops. Made Lieut. in 3rd. New Jersey Volunteers 21 Feb. 1777 (his own account claims he was a prisoner?) He died 20 April 1823, Parrsborough, Nova Scotia at age 89. Left a widow, son and two married daughters. Also listed in Gen. Skinner's Brigade muster roll in Seconded Officers (date unknown) at age 48 from America.
Source - HKC#2 & LNJR & GSB

FRASER, Neil (widow of)
The widow of Neil Fraser granted 250 acres in Douglas, Nova Scotia along with widow of Donald Fraser for serving in 2nd. Battalion, 84th. Regiment.
Source - WWRD

FRENCH, Adolphus Lieut.
Granted with other loyalist refugee's 21,380 acres by Gov. Parr 8 Aug. 1795(85?) in Kings County, Nova Scotia. Excheated 14 May 1814. Also listed in Gen. Skinner's Brigade muster roll, Seconded Officers (date unknown) at age 42 from America.
Source - HKC#3 & GSB

FRENCH, Albert
Listed as loyalist settler in Cornwall, Ontario in 1790's alone and on his land.
Source - LCO

FRENCH, Andrew
Listed with Sir John Johnston's Brigade and later joined Joseph Brant's Volunteers. Disbanded in 1783 and possibly granted land in Niagara, Ontario.
Source - SJJB

FRENCH, Benjamin
Listed as loyalist settler in Cornwall, Ontario in 1790's alone.
Source - LCO

FROST, John
Listed as Private on muster roll of Capt. Jonathan Randall's company in His Majesty's Loyal American Regiment commanded by Col. Beverly Robinson on 27 August 1778 (location unknown).
Source - DSR2

FROTZ, Henrick
Listed as Private in First Battalion, Kings Royal Rangers of New York 1775-77. From Turloch, Tryon County, New York. Possibly settled at Williamsburg, Ontario after 1783.
Source - SJJB

FRYZINER (Frysiner), John
Listed as a Private in 4th. Battalion New Jersey Volunteers muster roll commanded by Lt. Col. Abraham Bushkirk and Capt. Peter Ruton (Ruttan) at Staten Island, New York dated March 1778. Listed as Private and died 20 Jan. 1778. Also listed on 18 Nov. 1777 Muster at same place stating that he enlisted on 7 Dec. 1776. Again on 6 Jan. 1778 Muster at same place and sick at General Hospital. Again in March 1778 Muster at same place and listed as dead on 20 Jan. 1778.

Source - 4BNJVM & DSR

FRYZYNER (Frysiner) (Frisinor) (Frisener), Coenrad (Counrate) (Coonrod)
Listed as a Private in 4th. Battalion New Jersey Volunteers muster roll commanded by Lt. Col. Abraham Bushkirk and Capt. Peter Ruton (Ruttan) at Staten Island, New York dated March 1778. Listed as Private and sick in New York. Also listed on 18 Nov. 1777 Muster at same place stating that he enlisted on 7 Dec. 1776. Again on 6 Jan. 1778 Muster at same place and sick in General Hospital. Again in March and May and July 1778 Muster at same place and still sick in New York. And possibly August or September, October and 30 Dec. 1778 and Jan. 1779 Musters as a prisoner with the Rebels. On March 1779 Muster at Hobuck (Hoboken), New Jersey and at Powles Hook 7 July 1779 and again on August 1779 muster, but noted that he was taken prisoner on 19 Aug. 1779 and at Governor's Island on 29 Oct. and Dec. 1779 still prisoner. Also on 19 March and May 1780 muster (location unknown)(prisoner). On 14 July and 11 Sept. and 2 Dec. 1780 muster at Staten Island, New York (prisoner). Listed on 29 April 1781 muster at Staten Island (prisoner).
Source - 4BNJVM & DSR

FUKES, Daniel
Listed on muster roll of First Battalion of Maryland Loyalists 11 July 1778 at Long Island, New York. Enlisted 20 Dec. 1777.
Source - ML

FULLER, Daniel
Joined the Royal Standard 1777, listed in Kings American Regiment, Col. Fanning 1779. Possibly fled New Jersey in 1777. Died May 1822. Son was Isaac Fuller and John Fuller who also settled Niagara may be a son of Daniel. His wife was Charlotte whose probate record is dated 7 Sept. 1824 at Niagara. Daniel petitioned for 200 acres of wasteland of the Crown with his family in Niagara, Upper Canada 14 Dec. 1809 saying he lived in Saint John, New Brunswick before. He had a team of cattle, farming utensils for improving the land. There is also a Daniel in New Brunswick land petition between himself and Peter Clements in York County 1788. Daniel put in claims for losses from the war and received 89 pounds, 10 shilling (one record says for War of 1812, but probably is the Revolutionary War for being a loyalist?
Source - FLP

FULLER, Isaac
Born possibly in New Jersey/New York. Daniel Fuller was his father and they all fled to New Brunswick c.1783. Isaac moved to Niagara (Upper Canada) 1802. Petition government for 200 acres of the town's wasteland on 12 Dec. 1809, had team of cattle, farming utensils and was able to do the work. John Fox was witness.
Source - FLP

FULTON, James
A yeoman from Londonderry, NH. The New Hampshire General Assembly listed him and 75 others as the enemy in Nov. 1778.
Source - NHL

GAITS, Thomas
Listed with Sir John Johnston's Brigade and later joined Joseph Brant's Volunteers. Disbanded in 1783 and possibly granted land in Niagara, Ontario.
Source - SJJB

GARNET, Joseph Quartermaster
Listed on muster roll of First Battalion of Maryland Loyalists 11 July 1778 at Long Island, New York.
Source - ML

GARTER, John
From Tryon County, New York near the Mohawk River. Was a Tenant of Col. Claus. Taken prisoner in April 1780.
Source - HP

GARVEY, William
Listed as a Private on May 1783 Muster Roll of Lieut. Col. Stephen Delancey, commanded by Col. Cortland Skinner Esq. at New Town (location unclear).
Source - DMR

GERLOCH, Jacob
Listed as Private in First Battalion, Kings Royal Rangers of New York 1775-77. From Turloch, Tryon County, New York. Possibly settled at Williamsburg, Ontario after 1783.
Source - SJJB

GERLOCH, Peter
Listed as Private in First Battalion, Kings Royal Rangers of New York 1775-77. From Turloch, Tryon County, New York. Possibly settled at Williamsburg, Ontario after 1783.
Source - SJJB

GERMAN, Isaac
Listed as Private on muster roll of Capt. John Howard's company of New York Volunteers commanded by Lieut. Col. George Turnbull Esq., Commandant at Paulus Hook February 1778. And on muster of Capt. William Gray (same company) from 24 Feb. to 24 April 1781, location unknown.
Source - DSR3

GIANT, Jacob
Listed with Sir John Johnston's Brigade and later loined to Butler's Rangers. Disbanded in 1783 and possibly moved to Niagara, Ontario.
Source - SJJB

GIFFORD, Benjamin
Listed as Private on muster roll of Capt. John Howard's company of New York Volunteers commanded by Lieut. Col. George Turnbull Esq., Commandant at Paulus Hook, February 1778. Also listed on muster of Capt. William Gray (same company) from 24 Feb. to 24 April 1781, location unknown.
Source - DSR3

GIGG, John
Listed as Private on muster roll of Major Thomas Barclay's company in the Loyal American Regiment commanded by Col. Beverly Robinson at Guanus on 11 May 1782.
Source - DSR2

GILI (GILL?), William
Granted 200 acres at Nine-Mile River, ten miles west of Shubenacadie, Nova Scotia. Also is listed for getting 250 acres in Douglas, Nova Scotia for serving with 2nd. Battalion, 84th. Regiment. Also listed under Gill for getting 400 acres in Rawdon/Douglas under Major General Small.
Source - WWRD

GILLMORE, Robert
A yeoman from Keene, NH. The New Hampshire General assembly listed him and 75 others as the enemy in Nov. 1778.
Source - NHL

GISKINN, Charles
Listed as loyalist settler in Cornwall, Ontario in 1790's by himself.
Source - LCO

GOLDER, James
Listed as Private on muster roll of Capt. William Gray's company of New York Volunteers from 24 Feb. to 24 April 1781, location unknown.
Source - DSR3

GOLDER, William
Listed as Corporal on muster roll of Capt. William Gray's company of New York Volunteers from 24 Feb. to 24 April 1781, location unknown.
Source - DSR3

GOLLINGER, George
Listed as loyalist settler in Cornwall, Ontario in 1790's on his land.
Source LCO

GOLLINGER, Michael Sr.
Listed as loyalist settler in Cornwall, Ontario in 1790's with 3 dependants on his land.
Source - LCO

GOLLINGER, Michael Jr.
Listed as loyalist settler in Cornwall, Ontario in 1790's by himself.
Source - LCO

GOODSPEED, Isaiah
Was jailed in Sandwich, Massachusetts (Cape Cod) for being a loyalist in March 1778 per the Percival Diary located at Sandwich Archives.
Source - SA

GOODSPEED, Josiah
From Barnstable, Massachusetts (Cape Cod). Was a Yeoman. Found guilty in 1779 for a disloyal speech. Remained after the British left.
Source - DH

GORHAM, David
Born 6 April 1712 and died 27 Feb. 1786 in Barnstable, Massachusetts (Cape Cod). Educated at Harvard in 1733 and became an attorney, registrar of probate, justice of the peace, court clerk and colonel. He married first on 2 August 1733 to Abigail Sturges. His second wife, Elizabeth Cobb, daughter of James Cobb. And his third was Hannah Davis, daughter to James Davis. David's father was Col. Shubael Gorham and his mother was Mary Thatcher. They were mobbed for siding with the British, but did not leave.
Source - DH

GORHAM, Prince
From Barnstable, Massachusetts (Cape Cod). Was arrested in 1776, but remained after British left.
Source - DH

GOSS, Ann (Riddle)
Wife of loyalist Zachariah Goss and possible daughter to loyalist Col. James Riddle of Surry Co., North Carolina. Husband hanged in 1781. Her whereabouts not known.
Source - JWC

GOSS, Thomas
Loyalist from Granville County, North Carolina who disappears from there around 1771, but turns up in Pendleton District of South Carolina in 1794. Possibly rejoined the Patriot cause?
Source - JWC

GOSS, Zachariah
Was hanged at Wilkesboro, North Carolina in 1781 by Colonel Benjamin Cleveland. Possibly the son of Thomas Goss of Granville Co., North Carolina. Zachariah and his wife Ann sold their land in Granville Co., N.C. in 1771 and was never recorded in North Carolina after that. Ann could have been daughter of Loyalist, Col. James Riddle of Surry Co., N.C. (no proof yet).
Source - JWC

GOULD, Thomas
Master of the schooner, William. Was from Eastham (Cape Cod), Barnstable County, Massachusetts (Cape Cod). He took loyalist, John Prince of Salem, Massachusetts to Halifax, Nova Scotia on a whaling

voyage December 1774. In May 1775 Gould returned to see his family and vessel seized and his schooner hauled on shore and stripped of everything.
Source - ALC

GRANT, Donald
Granted 500 acres in Douglas, Nova Scotia for serving in 2nd. Battalion, 84th. Regiment.
Source - WWRD

GRANT, John
Granted 250 acres in Douglas, Nova Scotia for serving in 2nd. Battalion, 84th. Regiment.
Source - WWRD

GRANT, Peter
Granted 500 acres in Douglas, Nova Scotia for serving in 2nd. Battalion, 84th. Regiment.
Source - WWRD

GRANDY, David
Listed on muster roll of Capt. William Howison's Company of Loyal American Regiment in New York dated 24 Oct. 1780. He was a Private on guard.
Source - VNB

GRANDY, Joseph
Listed on 4,400 acre land grant with Thomas Green and others who were listed in the Royal Nova Scotia Volunteers at Ship Harbour, Halifax Co., Nova Scotia. He was a Corporal. This grant was dated 2 June 1784. He later removed to Cape Breton, Nova Scotia.
Source - VNB

GRATTON, Thomas
Listed on muster roll of First Battalion of Maryland Loyalists 11 July 1778 at Long Island, New York. Enlisted 4 Nov. 1777.
Source - ML

GRAY, William Capt.
Listed as Captain on his own muster roll of New York Volunteers from 24 Feb. to 24 April 1781, location unknown.
Source - DSR3

GREEN, ... Private
Granted land in Douglas, Nova Scotia 13 Dec. 1785 for service in 2nd. Battalion, 84th. Regiment.
Source - WWRD

GREEN, George
Listed in New Jersey Volunteers muster roll commanded under Col. Joseph Barton and Capt. James Shaw dated 12 Feb. 1777 (listed with William Green).
Source - NJM

GREEN, William
Listed in New Jersey Volunteers muster roll commanded under Col. Joseph Barton and Capt. James Shaw dated 17 Feb. 1777 and again on 12 Feb/6,8 & 12 March. 1777.
Source - NJM

GREENO, Allan
Granted 250 acres in Rawdon/Douglas, Nova Scotia under Major General Small.
Source - WWRD

GRIFFIE, John
Listed on muster roll of First Battalion of Maryland Loyalists 11 July 1778 at Long Island, New York. Enlisted 20 Dec. 1777 and on duty.
Source - ML

GRIFFIN, Obadiah
Listed as Private on recruiting duty on muster roll of Capt. John Howard's company of New York Volunteers commanded by Lieut. Col. George Turnbull Esq., Commandant at Paulus Hook, February 1778.
Source - DSR3

GRIFFIN, Thomas
Listed as Private on muster roll of Capt. John Howard's company of New York Volunteers commanded by Lieut. Col. George Turnbull Esq., Commandant at Paulus Hook, February 1778. Also on muster of Capt. William Gray (same company) from 24 Feb. to 24 April 1781, location unknown.
Source - DSR3

GRITMAN, John
Listed as Private on duty on muster roll of Capt. John Howard's company of New York Volunteers commanded by Lieut. Col. George Turnbull Esq., Commandant at Paulus Hook, February 1778. And again on muster of Capt. William Gray (same company) from 24 Feb. to 24 April 1781, location unknown.
Source - DSR3

GRITSMAN, John
Listed as Private in General Hospital on muster roll of Capt. William Gray's company of New York Volunteers from 24 Feb. to 24 April 1781, location unknown. The above John Gritman is also listed on same muster.
Source - DSR3

GRIZLI(?), Seth
Listed as a Private on muster roll of Capt. Christopher Hatch's Company of Loyal Americans, commanded by Col. Beverly Robinson at Haarlem, New York, possibly at beginning of 1778 and on 21 April 1778 muster.
Source - DSR2

GROFS, Jacob
Listed in New Jersey Volunteers muster roll commanded under Col. Joseph Barton and Capt. James Shaw dated 1 April 1777.
Source - NJM

HACKS, Stephen
Listed as Private on muster roll of Capt. Jonathan Randall's company in His Majesty's Loyal American Regiment commanded by Col. Beverly Robinson 27 August 1788 (location unknown).
Source - DSR2

HAGERTHY, Patrick
Late of Sussex County, New Jersey, listed in inquisition 9 Feb. 1779 at Court of Inquiry, Sussex by Isaac Martin and Samuel Meeker, Commissioners.
Source - NJNE

HAIGHT, William
Listed as Sergeant at Comm. Loyds Neck on muster roll of Capt. Jonathan Randall's company in His Majesty's Loyal American Regiment commanded by Col. Beverly Robinson on 27 August 1778.
Source - DSR2

HAINS, Urbanus
Listed with Sir John Johnston's Brigade and later joined Butler's Rangers. Disbanded in 1783 and possibly moved to Niagara, Ontario.
Source - SJJB

HALE, Samuel Jr. Esq.
Was listed as loyalist from New Hampshire. Followed Gov. John Wentworth of New Hampshire into exile to Flatbush, Long Island, New York around 1777. The New Hampshire General Assembly listed him and 75 others as the enemy in Nov. 1778 (this record did not say Jr.?).
Source - NHL

HALEY, George
Of the 44th. Regiment settled in Cornwall, Ontario in 1790's alone.
Source - LCO

HALL, Isaac
Listed as Private on Comm. at Loyds Neck on muster roll of Capt. Jonathan Randall's company in His Majesty's Loyal American Regiment commanded by Col. Beverly Robinson on 27 August 1778.
Source - DSR2

HALL, Uriah
Listed as Private on recruiting duty on muster roll of Capt. John Howard's company of New York Volunteers commanded by Lieut. Col. George Turnbull Esq., Commandant at Paulus Hook, February 1778.
Source - DSR3

HALLENBECK, Aaron
Listed with Sir John Johnston's Brigade and later joined Joseph Brant's Volunteers. Disbanded in 1783 and possibly granted land in Niagara, Ontario.
Source - SJJB

HALMER, John
From Tryon County, New York near the Mohawk river and was tenant of Col. Claus. Taken prisoner in April 1780.
Source - HP

HAMBLETON, Andrew
Listed as Private in First Battalion of Kings Royal Rangers, New York 1775-77. From Turloch, Tryon County, New York. Possibly settled at Williamsburg, Ontario after 1783.
Source - SJJB

HAMBLETON, Robert
Listed as Private in First Battalion, Kings Royal Rangers of New York 1775-77. From Turloch, Tryon County, New York. Possibly settled at Williamsburg, Ontario after 1783.
Source - SJJB

HANCOCK, Joseph
Listed in New Jersey Volunteers muster roll commanded under Col. Joseph Barton and Capt. James Shaw dated 17 Feb./2 March & 20 March 1777 (twice on 1 March 1777).
Source - NJM

HANDLY (Handley), Sylvester
Listed as Private on muster roll in Capt. John Howard's company of New York Volunteers commanded by Lieut. Col. George Turnbull Esq., Commandant at Paulus Hook, February 1778. Also listed on muster of Capt. William Gray (same muster) from 24 Feb. to 24 April 1781, location unknown.
Source - DSR3

HANNA, John
Listed as Private in First Battalion of Kings Royal Rangers of New York 1775-77. From Turloch, Tryon County, New York. Possibly settled at Williamsburg, Ontario after 1783.
Source - SJJB

HANSELPECKER, Coenrad (Counrate)
Listed in 4th. Battalion New Jersey Volunteers muster roll commanded by Lt. Col. Abraham Bushkirk and Capt. Peter Ruton (Ruttan)at Staten Island, New York dated March 1778. Listed as Private and a Carpenter. Also listed on 6 Jan. 1778 Muster at same place and on command. Again in March and May (Taylor at Harlem) and July (on command at New York) 1778 Muster at same place and as on command as Carpenter. Listed again in possibly August or September and October and 30 Dec. 1778 Muster at same place but it say again that he was a Taylor at Harlem. Also turns up on Muster dated Jan. 1779 (place not clear). On

March 1779 Muster at Hobuck (Hoboken), New Jersey and at Powles Hook 7 July 1779, still a Taylor at Harlem and again on August 1779 muster in same company and at Governor's Island on 29 Oct. and Dec. (on Furlow)1779. Also on 19 March and May 1780 muster (location unknown). On 14 July and 11 Sept. and 2 Dec. 1780 muster at Staten Island, New York. Listed on 29 April 1781 muster at Staten Island.
Source - 4BNJVM & DSR

HANSELPECKER (Henselbecker), Philip
Listed in 4th. Battalion New Jersey Volunteers muster roll commanded by Lt. Col. Abraham Bushkirk and Capt. Peter Ruton (Ruttan) at Staten Island, New York dated March and July (on Guard) 1778. Listed as Private. Also listed on 6 Jan. 1778 Muster at same place on (C.M. Command). Again in March and May and possibly August or September and October 1778 as a Corporal Muster at same place. Again on 30 Dec. 1778 and on Jan. 1779 (place unknown). On March 1779 Muster at Hobuck (Hoboken), New Jersey and at Powles Hook 7 July 1779 listed as Corporal. On possible August 1779 Muster (location unknown) and at Governor's Island on 29 Oct. 1779 and Dec. 1779. Also on 19 March and May 1780 muster (location unknown). On 14 July and 11 Sept. and 2 Dec. 1780 muster at Staten Island, New York. Listed on 29 April 1781 muster at Staten Island.
Source - 4BNJVM & DSR

HANSELPECKER, William
Listed in 4th. Battalion New Jersey Volunteers muster roll commanded by Lt. Col. Abraham Bushkirk and Capt. Peter Ruton at Staten Island, New York dated March 1778. Listed as Private and discharged.
Source - 4BNJVM & DSR

HARRIOTT, Thomas
Granted with other refugee loyalist's 21, 380 acres by Gov. Parr 8 Aug. 1795 (85?) in Kings County, Nova Scotia.
Source - HKC#3

HARRIS, John
Settled Annapolis, Nova Scotia and was an agent and member of the land board for Digby, NS 1783-84.
Source - NHL

HART, Benjamin
Gave permission to leave New Hampshire at Portsmouth on a flag of truce transport with his family for Rhode Island on 8 Oct. 1777. Was a rope maker. New Hampshire General Assembly listed him and 75 others as the enemy in Nov. 1778. His home was at Portsmouth, NH.
Source - NHL

HART, Joseph
Listed as a Private in Capt. Peter Ruton's Company in the 4th. Battalion of New Jersey Volunteers commanded by Lieut. Col. Abraham Bushkirk at Staten Island, New York in May, July and possibly August or September, October and 30 Dec. 1778.
Source - DSR

HARTER, Charles
Listed on muster roll of First Battalion of Maryland Loyalists 11 July 1778 at Long Island, New York. Enlisted 6 Nov. 1777.
Source - ML

HASTINGS, Joseph Stacy (Stacey)
Listed as loyalist from New Hampshire. He was a Harvard graduate of 1762 and fled to Halifax, Nova Scotia, but returned to Boston where he started a grocery store. He probably left there soon after.
Source - NHL

HATCH, Christopher Captain
Listed as Captain on his muster roll of Loyal Americans, commanded by Col. Beverly Robinson at Haarlem, New York, possibly beginning of 1778 and on 21 April 1778 muster.
Source - DSR2

HATFIELD, Thomas
Listed as Private on muster roll of Capt. John Howard's company of New York Volunteers commanded by Lieut. Col. George Turnbull Esq., Commandant at Paulus Hook, February 1778.
Source - DSR3

HATHAWAY, Luther Lieut.
Granted with other refugee loyalists 21, 380 acres by Gov. Parr 8 Aug. 1795 (85?) in Kings County, Nova Scotia.
Source - HKC#3

HAUCHS, John
Listed in Turloch, Tryon County, New York Militia 1775-77 and later in Butler's Rangers.
Source - SJJB

HAWKINS, Samuel
Listed as Private on muster roll of Capt. John Howard's company of New York Volunteers commanded by Lieut. Col. George Turnbull Esq., Commandant at Paulus Hook, February 1778.
Source - DSR3

HAWLEY, Johekud
Listed with Sir John Johnston's Brigade and later joined Joseph Brant's Volunteers. Disbanded in 1783 and possibly granted land in Niagara, Ontario.
Source - SJJB

HAWS, William
Listed as Private who died 3 August 1777 on muster roll of Capt. William Gray's company of New York Volunteers from 24 Feb. to 24 April 1781, location unknown.
Source - DSR3

HAY, Cornelius
Listed as Sergeant on muster roll of Major Thomas Barclay's company in the Loyal American Regiment commanded by Col. Beverly Robinson at Guanus on 11 May 1782.
Source - DSR2

HAYNER, James
Listed as Private on muster roll of Capt. William Gray's company of New York Volunteers from 24 Feb. to 24 April 1781, location unknown.
Source - DSR3

HAYS, John
Listed as Private who deserted on 26 Aug. 1777 on muster roll of Capt. William Gray's company of New York Volunteers from 24 Feb. to 24 April 1781, location unknown.
Source - DSR3

HECKE, John

Listed in Turloch, Tryon County, New York Militia, 1775-77 and later joined the Kings Royal Rangers of New York.
Source - SJJB

HEMMEUM (Hemeon)(Himmeum), Adam (Adem)
Listed in 4th. Battalion New Jersey Volunteers muster roll commanded by Lt. Col. Abraham Bushkirk and Capt. Peter Ruton (Ruttan) at Staten Island, New York dated March 1778. Listed as Private and sick in New York. Also listed on 18 Nov. 1777 Muster at same place as deserted. He enlisted on 7 Dec. 1776. Again listed on 6 Jan. 1778 Muster at same place and still sick at General Hospital. Again in March and May and July and possibly August or September (on Furlow) 1778 Muster at same place still sick in New York.
Source - 4BNJVM & DSR

HEMMEUM (Hemeon)(Hemion)(Himmion), George
Listed as a Private in 4th. Battalion New Jersey Volunteers muster roll commanded by Lt. Col. Abraham Bushkirk and Capt. Peter Ruton (Ruttan) at Staten Island, New York dated March 1778. Listed as Carpenter. Also listed on 18 Nov. 1777 at same place as on guard and who enlisted on 7 Dec. 1776. Again listed on 6 Jan. 1778 Muster at same place. Again in March and May (sick in quarters) and July 1778 Muster at same place and as a Carpenter. Possibly on Muster of August or September, October and 30 Dec. 1778. And again on Muster dated Jan. 1779 (place not clear). On March 1779 Muster at Hobuck (Hoboken), New Jersey and at Powles Hook 7 July 1779. On possible August 1779 Muster (place unknown) and at Governor's Island on 29 Oct. 1779 and Dec. 1779. Also on 19 March and May 1780 muster (location unknown). On 14 July and 11 Sept. and 2 Dec. 1780 muster at Staten Island, New York. Listed on 29 April 1781 muster at Staten Island.
Source - 4BNJVM & DSR

HEMMEUM, Henry
Listed in 4th. Battalion New Jersey Volunteers muster roll commanded by Lt. Col. Abraham Bushkirk and Capt. Peter Ruton at Staten Island, New York dated March 1778. Listed as Private and discharged.
Source - 4BNJVM & DSR

HEMMEUM (Hemeon)(Hemion)(Himmion), Jacob
Listed as a Private in 4th. Battalion New Jersey Volunteers muster roll commanded by Lt. Col. Abraham Bushkirk and Capt. Peter Ruton (Ruttan) at Staten Island, New York dated March 1778. Listed Carpenter

too. Also listed on 18 Nov. 1777 Muster at same place as Sick and in the General Hospital. It states that he enlisted on 7 Dec. 1776. Again listed on 6 Jan. 1778 Muster at same place. Again in March and May and July 1778 Muster at same place and as a Carpenter. Again listed on possibly August or September, October and 30 Dec. 1778 Muster. And again on Jan. 1779 Muster (place not known). On March 1779 Muster at Hobuck (Hoboken), New Jersey and at Powles Hook 7 July 1779. On possible August 1779 Muster (place unknown) and at Governor's Island on 29 Oct. 1779 and Dec. 1779. Also on 19 March and May 1780 muster (location unknown). On 14 July and 11 Sept. and 2 Dec. 1780 muster at Staten Island, New York. Listed on 29 April 1781 muster at Staten Island.
Source - 4BNJVM & DSR

HEMMEUM (Hemeon)(Himmeum)(Hemion), Nicholas (Nicholass)
Listed as a Private in 4th. Battalion New Jersey Volunteers muster roll commanded by Lt. Col. Abraham Bushkirk and Capt. Peter Ruton (Ruttan) at Staten Island, New York dated March 1778. Listed as Private. Also listed on 18 Nov. 1777 Muster at same place stating that he enlisted on 7 Dec. 1776. Again listed on 6 Jan. 1778 Muster at same place and sick at General Hospital. Again in March, May and July and possibly August or September, October and 30 Dec. 1778 Muster at same place. Also listed on Muster of Jan. 1779 (place unknown). On March 1779 Muster at Hobuck (Hoboken), New Jersey. On possible August 1779 Muster (place unknown) and at Governor's Island on 29 Oct. 1779 and Dec. 1779. Also on 19 March and May 1780 muster (location unknown). On 14 July and 11 Sept. and 2 Dec. 1780 muster at Staten Island, New York. Listed on 29 April 1781 muster at Staten Island.
Source - 4BNJVM & DSR

HENDERSON, Calib
Listed with Sir John Johnston's Brigade and later joined Joseph Brant's Volunteers. Disbanded in 1783 and possibly granted land in Niagara, Ontario.
Source - SJJB

HENDERSON, Hugh
A Merchant. New Hampshire General Assembly listed him and 75 others as the enemy in Nov. 1778. His home at Portsmouth, NH.
Source - NHL

HENNIGAR, Christian

Granted 500 acres in Douglas, Nova Scotia for serving in 2nd. Battalion, 84th. Regiment. Also listed as getting 1000 and 500 acres in Rawdon/Douglas, Nova Scotia under Major General Small.
Source - WWRD

HENRIQUES, Philip
Listed as a Private on Muster Roll of Capt. Peter Ruton's Company in the 4th. Battalion of New Jersey Volunteers commanded by Lieut. Col. Abraham Buskirk at Hobuck (Hoboken), New Jersey in March 1779. Also listed at Powles Hook 7 July 1779 and again on possible August 1779 Muster (place unknown) stating that he deserted 15/16 July 1779 and listed again in Dec. 1779 as returning from desertion on 9 Nov. 1779.
Source - DSR

HENRY, Patrick Lieut.
Granted with other refugee loyalist's 21, 380 acres by Gov. Parr 8 Aug. 1795 (85?) in Kings County, Nova Scotia. Also listed in Gen. Skinner's Brigade muster roll in Seconded Officers (date unknown) at age 55 from Ireland.
Source - HKC#3 & GSB

HENTZ, Henrick
Served in Turloch, Tryon County, New York Militia 1775-77 and later in Kings Royal Rangers of New York.
Source - SJJB

HEREFORD (?), Charles
Listed as Drummer on muster roll of Capt. John Howard's company of New York Volunteers commanded by Lieut. Col. George Turnbull Esq., Commandant at Paulus Hook, February 1778.
Source - DSR3

HERKNER, Nicelas
Listed with Sir John Johnston's Brigade and later joined Joseph Brant's Volunteers. Disbanded in 1783 and possibly granted land in Niagara, Ontario.
Source - SJJB

HESS(?), Michael
Listed as a Private in May 1783 Muster Roll of Lieut. Col. Stephen Delancey, commanded by Cortland Skinner Esq. at New Town (location unclear).

Source - DMR

HETFIELD, John Capt.
Granted with others 8,900 acres 15 Oct. 1784 by Gov. Parr in Kings County, Nova Scotia.
Source - HKC#2

HIGBY, George
Listed as Private on muster roll of Capt. Christopher Hatch's Company of Loyal Americans, commanded by Col. Beverly Robinson at Haarlem, New York, possibly beginning of 1778 and on 21 April 1778 muster.
Source - DSR2

HILL, James
Listed as Private on muster roll in Capt. Jonathan Randall's company in His Majesty's Loyal American Regiment commanded by Col. Beverly Robinson on 27 August 1778 (location unknown).
Source - DSR2

HILL, Richard
Member of the land board of Digby, Nova Scotia 1783-4.
Source - NHL

HILL, Timothy
Listed with Sir John Johnston's Brigade and later joined Joseph Brant's Volunteers. Disbanded in 1783 and possibly granted land in Niagara, Ontario.
Source - SJJB

HILL, Zachariah
Listed as Private on muster roll of Capt. Jonathan Randall's company in His Majesty's Loyal American Regiment commanded by Col. Beverly Robinson on 27 August 1778 (location unknown).
Source - DSR2

HOBBER, Abraham
Listed in Turloch, Tryon County, New York Militia 1775-77 and later in the Kings Royal Rangers of New York.
Source - SJJB

HOFFMAN, Christian
Listed in New Jersey Volunteers muster roll commanded by Col. Joseph Barton and Capt. James Shaw dated 26 Jan. 1777.
Source - NJM

HOFFMAN, George
Listed in New Jersey Volunteers muster roll commanded under Col. Joseph Barton and Capt. James Shaw dated 1 April 1777 (Christian Hoffman listed on 26 Jan. 1777 list).
Source - NJM

HOFFMAN, Nicholas
Late of Morris County, New Jersey was listed in Court of Inquiry 9 Feb. 1779 (inquisition) with others in Sussex County, NJ by Isaac Martin and Samuel Meeker, Commissioners.
Source - NJNE

HOGATEALING, Aaron
Listed with Sir John Johnston's Brigade and later joined Butler's Rangers. Disbanded in 1783 and possibly granted land in Niagara, Ontario.
Source - SJJB

HOGLAND, Obadiah
Listed in New Jersey Volunteers muster roll commanded by Col. Joseph Barton and Capt. James Shaw dated 1 March 1777.
Source - NJM

HOLLAND, Henry
Listed as a Private on May 1783 Muster Roll of Lieut. Col. Stephen Delancey, commanded by Col. Cortland Skinner Esq. at New Town (location unclear).
Source - DMR

HOLLAND, John
A gentleman from Amherst, NH. The New Hampshire General Assembly listed him and 75 others as the enemy in Nov. 1778. He settled at Saint John, New Brunswick and became sheriff of that county.
Source - NHL

HOLLAND, Richard
A yeoman from Londonderry, NH. The New Hampshire General Assembly listed him and 75 others as the enemy in Nov. 1778. Stephen Holland Esq. listed with him.
Source - NHL

HOLLAND, Samuel Esq.
New Hampshire General Assembly listed him with 75 others as the enemy in Nov. 1778. His home was at Portsmouth, NH. On confiscation list of 28 Nov. 1778.
Source - NHL

HOLLAND, Stephen Esq.
A gentleman from Londonderry, NH. The New Hampshire General Assembly listed him with 75 others as the enemy in Nov. 1778. Richard Holland from same place listed with him. On confiscation list of 28 Nov. 1778. Was a member of the Prince of Wales American Volunteers.
Source - NHL

HOLLANT, Davit
Listed in Turloch, Tryon County, New York Militia 1775-77 and later in the Kings Royal Rangers of New York.
Source - SJJB

HOPPER, Garret
Listed as a Corporal on Muster Roll of Capt. Peter Ruttan's Company in the 4th. Battalion of New Jersey Volunteers commanded by Lieut. Col. Abraham Buskirk Esq. At Staten Island, New York.
Source - DSR

HOPPER, John Sergeant
Listed in 4th. Battalion New Jersey Volunteers muster roll commanded by Lt. Col. Abraham Bushkirk and Capt. Peter Ruton (Ruttan) at Staten Island, New York dated March 1778. Also listed on 18 Nov. 1777 Muster at same place as a Private who enlisted on 22 April 1777. Again on 6 Jan. 1778 Muster at same place, but sick in General Hospital. Again in March, May and July and possibly August or September and October (as Corporal) 1778 Muster at same place. Again on 30 Dec. 1778. Listed again as Corporal and on the ship, Sloop Nipten Jan. 1779. On March 1779 Muster at Hobuck (Hoboken), New Jersey and at Powles Hook (sick in quarters) 7 July 1779. On possible August 1779 Muster (location unknown) and at Governor's Island on 29 Oct. 1779 and Dec. 1779. Also

on 19 March and May 1780 muster (location unknown). On 14 July and 11 Sept. and 2 Dec. 1780 muster at Staten Island, New York. Listed on 29 April 1781 muster at Staten Island, but noted that he was "on board the Sloop Neptune".
Source - 4BNJVM & DSR

HORNING, John
Listed in Turloch, Tryon County, New York Militia 1775-77 and later in the Kings Royal Rangers of New York.
Source - SJJB

HORRICK, Nicholas
Listed in 4th. Battalion New Jersey Volunteers muster roll commanded by Lt. Col. Abraham Bushkirk and Capt. Peter Ruton at Staten Island, New York dated March 1778. Listed as Private and discharged.
Source - 4BNJVM & DSR

HOUADORNE, Peter
Listed as Private on muster roll of Capt. John Howard's company of New York Volunteers commanded by Lieut. Col. George Turnbull Esq., Commandant at Paulus Hook, February 1778.
Source - DSR3

HOUSTON, William Mate
Listed on muster roll of First Battalion of Maryland Loyalists 11 July 1778 at Long Island, New York.
Source - ML

HOWARD, John Capt.
Listed on muster roll as Captain of his own company of New York Volunteers commanded by Lieut. Col. George Turnbull Esq., Commandant at Paulus Hook, February 1778.
Source - DSR3

HOWE (?), ...?
Listed as Sergeant on muster roll of Capt. John Howard's company of New York Volunteers commanded by Lieut. Col. George Turnbull Esq., Commandant at Paulus Hook, February 1778.
Source - DSR3

HOWK, Christian
Listed with Sir. John Johnston's Brigade and later joined Joseph Brant's Volunteers. Disbanded in 1783 and possibly granted land in Niagara, Ontario, Canada.
Source - SJJB

HOWLAND, Nathaniel
Was imprisoned in Boston for being a loyalist, escaped, was recaptured in Sandwich, Mass. (Cape Cod) in July 1779 per the Percival Diary.
Source - SA

HUBER, Adam
Listed in Turloch, Tryon County, New York Militia 1775-77 and later in the Kings Royal Rangers of New York.
Source - SJJB

HUGHES, Terrence
Listed on muster roll of First Battalion of Maryland Loyalists 11 July 1778 at Long Island, New York. Enlisted 6 Nov. 1777.
Source - ML

HUNT, Cosby
Listed as Lieutenant on muster roll of Capt. William Gray's company of New York Volunteers from 24 Feb. to 24 April 1781, location unknown.
Source - DSR3

HUTCHISON, William Lieutenant
Listed in New Jersey Volunteers muster roll commanded by Col. Joseph Barton and Capt. James Shaw dated 4 & 30 Jan. and 1 March 1777 (3 times on 26 Jan. 1777).
Source - NJM

JACKSON,............ Private
Granted land 13 Dec. 1785 in Douglas, Nova Scotia for service in 2nd. Battalion, 84th. Regiment.
Source - WWRD

JACKSON, Samuel
Listed as Private on muster roll of Capt. John Howard's company of New York Volunteers commanded by Lieut. Col. George Turnbull Esq., Commandant at Paulus Hook, February 1778.
Source - DSR3

JACKSON, Stephen
Listed as Private on muster roll of Capt. John Howard's company of New York Volunteers commanded by Lieut. Col. George Turnbull Esq., Commandant at Paulus Hook, February 1778.
Source - DSR3

JAICOCKS (Jeacox), David
Listed as Private on muster roll of Capt. John Howard's company of New York Volunteers commanded by Lieut. Col. George Turnbull Esq., Commandant at Paulus Hook, February 1778. Listed again on muster of Capt. William Gray (same company) from 24 Feb. to 24 April 1781, location unknown. A David Jeacocks is also listed on Gray's muster.
Source - DSR3

JAMES, John
Listed as Private at Comm. Loyds Neck on muster roll of Capt. Jonathan Randall's company in His Majesty's Loyal American Regiment commanded by Col. Beverly Robinson on 27 August 1778.
Source - DSR2

JAMES, John (Jr.?)
Listed as Drummer at Comm. Loyds Neck on muster roll of Capt. Jonathan Randall's company in His Majesty's Loyal American Regiment commanded by Col. Beverly Robinson on 27 August 1778.
Source - DSR2

JEACOCKS, David
Listed as Private on muster roll of Capt. William Gray's company of New York Volunteers from 24 Feb. to 24 April 1781, location unknown. A David Jeacox is also listed.
Source - DSR3

JENNINGS, John
Was labeled a loyalist and removed to New Brunswick, Canada with the other loyalist who settled that area in 1783. He was from Sandwich, Massachusetts (Cape Cod). He was jailed at the Barnstable goal for being a loyalist.
Source - SA

JEWELL, William
Listed as Private on muster roll of Major Thomas Barclay's company in the Loyal American Regiment commanded by Col. Beverly Robinson at Guanus on 11 May 1782.
Source - DSR2

JOHN(?), Peter
Listed as a Private on May 1783 Muster Roll of Lieut. Col. Stephen Delancey, commanded by Col. Cortland Skinner Esq. at New Town (location unclear).
Source - DMR

JOHNSON, Robert
Listed in New Jersey Volunteers muster roll commanded by Col. Joseph Barton and Capt. James Shaw dated 2 March 17777.
Source - NJM

JOHNSTONE, (Mral?), Surgeon
Listed in Gen. Skinner's muster roll, Seconded Officers (date unknown).
Source - GSB

JONES, Elijah (Elisha)
Listed as Private on muster roll of Capt. John Howard's company of New York Volunteers commanded by Lieut. Col. George Turnbull Esq., Commandant at Paulus Hook, February 1778. He was also listed with another Elijah Jones? Listed again on muster of Capt. William Gray (same company) from 24 Feb. to 24 April 1781, location unknown.
Source - DSR3

JONES (?), Elijah Sr.
Listed as Private on muster roll of Capt. John Howard's company of New York Volunteers commanded by Lieut. Col. George Turnbull Esq., Commandant at Paulus Hook, February 1778. Listed again on muster of Capt. William Gray (same company) from 24 Feb. to 24 April 1781, location unknown.
Source - DSR3

JONES, John
From Falmouth, Maine or Massachusetts? Was a mariner and was jailed in 1779 for supplying Great Britain. He remained after British left.
Source - DH

JONES, John
Listed as Private on muster roll of Capt. John Howard's company of New York Volunteers commanded by Lieut. Col. George Turnbull Esq., Commandant at Paulus Hook, February 1778. Also listed on muster of Capt. William Gray (same muster) from 24 Feb. to 24 April 1781, location unknown.
Source - DSR3

JONES, Joseph
Listed as a Private on muster roll of Capt. Christopher Hatch's Company of Loyal Americans, commanded by Col. Beverly Robinson at Haarlem, New York, possibly the beginning of 1778 and on 21 April 1778 muster.
Source - DSR2

JONES, Josiah
A gentleman from Hinsdale, NH. The New Hampshire General Assembly listed him and 75 others as the enemy in Nov. 1778 (listed with Simon Jones). On petition to change Conway to Digby, Nova Scotia in honor of Rear Admiral Robert Digby 20 Feb. 1784. Later, he settled at Weymouth, which was 17 miles south of Digby.
Source - NHL

JONES, Simeon
Was jailed in Sandwich, Massachusetts (Cape Cod) in March 1778 per the Percival Diary.
Source - SA

JONES, Simon
A gentleman from Hinsdale, NH (with Josiah Jones). The New Hampshire General Assembly listed him and 75 others as the enemy in Nov. 1778.
Source - NHL

JOUET, Cavilear
Late of Elizabeth Town, Sussex County, New Jersey, listed in inquisition 9 Feb. 1779 by Court of Inquiry by Isaac Martin and Samuel Meeker, Commissioners.
Source - NJNE

KEENE, Moses
Was labeled a loyalist in Sandwich, Massachusetts (Cape Cod), but stayed per Betsey Keene.
Source - SA

KENT, Samuel
Listed as a Private on muster roll of Capt. Christopher Hatch's Company of Loyal Americans, commanded by Col. Beverly Robinson at Haarlem, New York, possibly at beginning of 1778. It is noted that he died 20 April 1777, but still listed on 21 April 1778 muster as dead.
Source - DSR2

KERMISON, Jude
A Mariner. New Hampshire General Assembly listed him and 75 others as the enemy in Nov. 1778. His home was at Portsmouth, NH.
Source - NHL

KERSHAW, Henry
Listed as Private on muster roll of Capt. William Gray's company of New York Volunteers from 24 Feb. to 24 April 1781, location unknown.
Source - DSR3

KING, Benjamin
Listed as a Private on May 1783 Muster Roll of Lieut. Col. Stephen Delancey, commanded by Col. Cortland Skinner Esq. at New Town (location unclear).
Source - DMR

KING, James
Listed on muster roll of First Battalion of Maryland Loyalists 11 July 1778 at Long Island, New York. Enlisted 14 Nov. 1777.
Source - ML

KING, Samuel Corporal
Listed on muster roll of First Battalion of Maryland Loyalists 11 July 1778 at Long Island, New York. Enlisted 10 Dec. 1777.
Source - ML

KIPP, Isaac Major
Granted with other refugee's 21,380 acres by Gov. Parr 8 Aug. 1795(85?) in Kings County, Nova Scotia.
Source - HKC#3

KNEGT (Knaulgh)(Knought)(Kneght), Matthew Sergeant
Listed in 4th. Battalion New Jersey Volunteers muster roll commanded by Lt. Col. Abraham Bushkirk and Capt. Peter Ruton (Ruttan) at Staten Island, New York dated March 1778. Also listed on 18 Nov. 1777 Muster

as a Private at same place as taken prisoner on 29 Dec. 1776. He enlisted on 7 Dec. 1776. Again on 6 Jan. 1778 Muster, same place. Again in March and May and July (with the Artillery) and possibly August or September 1778 Muster at same place. Listed again on October 1778 and who enlisted 6 Dec. 1776, taken prisoner 26 Dec. 1777 with note; Not subsisted from 6 Dec. 1776 to 24 Dec. 1777. Listed again on 30 Dec. 1778 Muster at same place. On March 1779 Muster at Hobuck (Hoboken), New Jersey and at Powles Hook 7 July 1779. On possible August 1779 Muster (place unknown) and at Governor's Island on 29 Oct. 1779 listed as sick in the hospital and on Dec. 1779 saying that he "Has not drawn his bounty, and sick in New York". Also on 19 March 1780 muster (location unknown) as dead 22 Jan. 1780.
Source - 4BNJVM & DSR

KNOWLES, Isaac
From Sandwich, Barnstable County, Massachusetts (Cape Cod). Cited by town or committee of correspondence for being a Tory. He was jailed in 1778 at the Barnstable goal, but remained after British left.
Source - DH & SA

KRAMER, John
Listed in Turloch, Tryon County, New York Militia 1775-77 and then in the Kings Royal Rangers of New York.
Source - SJJB

KRENTHAL(?), John
Listed as Private on muster roll of Capt. Christopher Hatch's Company of Loyal Americans, commanded by Col. Beverly Robinson at Haarlem, New York, possibly beginning of 1778.
Source - DSR2

KRONK, John
Listed as Private on muster roll of Capt. Christopher Hatch's Company of Loyal Americans, commanded by Col. Beverly Robinson, possibly at Haarlem, New York on 21 April 1778.
Source - DSR2

KRONK(?), Timothy
Listed as Private on muster roll of Capt. Christopher Hatch's Company of Loyal Americans, commanded by Col. Beverly Robinson at Haarlem, New York, possibly at beginning of 1778 and on 21 April 1778 muster.
Source - DSR2

LABOTT(?), Raphael
Listed as a Private in May 1783 Muster Roll of Lieut. Col. Stephen Delancey, commanded by Col. Cortland Skinner Esq. at New Town (location unclear).
Source - DMR

LABY (Maby?), Peter
Listed as Private on muster roll of Capt. Christopher Hatch's Company of Loyal Americans, commanded by Col. Beverly Robinson at Haarlem, New York, possibly beginning 1778 and on 21 April 1778, on Barrack Guard duty.
Source - DSR2

LAFFIN, Thomas
Granted 500 acres in Douglas, Nova Scotia for serving in 2nd. Battalion, 84th. Regiment. Also listed as getting 700 acres in Rawdon/Douglas, Nova Scotia under Major General Small.
Source - WWRD

LALUTE, Peter
Listed on muster roll of First Battalion of Maryland Loyalists 11 July 1778 at Long Island, New York. Enlisted 6 Nov. 1777. Was sick in hospital.
Source - ML

LAMBERT, Sanistil(?)
Listed as a Private on May 1783 Muster Roll of Lieut. Col. Stephen Delancey, commanded by Col. Cortland Skinner Esq. at New Town (location unclear).
Source - DMR

LANGDON, Woodbury
A Portsmouth, New Hampshire and member of the Provincial Congress and not wanting to take sides, he fled with his family for England in October 1775. Lord North said on 7 Feb. 1777 that Woodbury had left America after using his influence for peace and good order to no avail.
Source - NHL

LAPSLIE, James
Listed as Private and confined with the Rebels on muster roll of Major Thomas Barclay's company in the Loyal American Regiment commanded by Col. Beverly Robinson at Guanus on 11 May 1782.
Source - DSR2

LAWBACK (Laubuck)(Lawbock)(Laubock), Henry (Henery)
Listed in 4th. Battalion New Jersey Volunteers muster roll commanded by Lt. Col. Abraham Bushkirk and Capt. Peter Ruton (Ruttan) at Staten Island, New York dated March and May 1778. Listed as Private and prisoner by rebels. Also listed on 18 Nov. 1777 Muster at same place as taken prisoner on 29 Dec. 1776. He enlisted on 7 Dec. 1776. Again listed on 6 Jan. and July and possibly August or September and October 1778 Muster at same place and still prisoner and on Jan. 1779 (location unknown). Listed again on August 1779 muster, but noted that he was taken prisoner before last muster and at Governor's Island on 29 Oct. and Dec. 1779 still prisoner. Also on 19 March and May 1780 muster (location unknown)(prisoner). On 14 July and 11 Sept. and 2 Dec. 1780 muster at Staten Island, New York (prisoner). Listed on 29 April 1781 muster at Staten Island (prisoner).
Source - 4BNJVM & DSR

LAWRENCE, Elisha Lieut. Col.
Granted with others 21,380 acres by Gov. Parr in Kings County, Nova Scotia 8 Aug. 1795(85?). Listed in Gen. Skinner's Brigade as from America and age 42 (date unknown)
Source - HKC#3 & GSB

LAWRENCE, John
Listed as lieutenant, but absent on May 1783 Muster Roll of Lieut. Col. Stephen Delancey at New Town (location no visible).
Source - DMR

LAWRENCE, Richard
Listed as Private on muster roll of Capt. John Howard's company of New York Volunteers commanded by Lieut. Col. George Turbull Esq., Commandant at Paulus Hook, February 1778. Listed again on muster of Capt. William Gray (same company) from 24 Feb. to 24 April 1781, location unknown.
Source - DSR3

LAWRENCE, Richard
Listed as Private, in General Hospital (two Richard's listed) on muster roll of Capt. William Gray's company of New York Volunteers from 24 Feb. to 24 April 1781, location unknown.
Source - DSR3

LEEDS(?), Daniel
Listed as a Private on May 1783 Muster Roll of Lieut. Col. Stephen Delancey, commanded by Col. Cortland Skinner Esq. at New Town (location unclear).
Source - DMR

LEHY, John
Granted 1000 acres at Five-Mile River, Nova Scotia under Major General Small.
Source - WWRD

LEONALD, Thomas Major
Listed in Gen. Skinner's Brigade muster roll of Seconded Officers (date unknown) at age 68 from America serving with the Provincials 7 1/2 years.
Source - GSB

LEROY, John
Listed as Private on muster roll of Major Thomas Barclay's company in the Loyal American Regiment commanded by Col. Beverly Robinson at Guanus on 11 May 1782.
Source - DSR2

LEWICK (Levick), Caleb
Listed as a Private on Muster Roll of Capt. Peter Rutton's Company in the 4th. Battalion of New Jersey Volunteers commanded by Lieut. Col. Abraham Buskirk (Bushkirk) at Staten Island, New York possibly August or September and October 1778. He enlisted on 27 July 1778. On March 1779 Muster at Hobuck (Hoboken), New Jersey and at Powles Hook 7 July 1779 and again on August 1779 muster and noted that he deserted.
Source - DSR

LEWICK, Philip
Listed as a Private on Muster Roll of Capt. Peter Rutton's Company in the 4th. Battalion of New Jersey Volunteers commanded by Lieut. Col. Abraham Buskirk at Staten Island, New York 30 Dec. 1778.
Source - DSR

LEWIS, Henry Phillip
Born c. 1760. Filed petition for land for loyalist service and was listed as being a native of Virginia, possibly Norfolk. Signed up with the Royal North Carolina Regiment in Feb. 1781 at Hillsborough, North Carolina

under Lieut. Col. John Hamilton. At the surrender of Yorktown on 19 Oct. 1781, Private Lewis sailed on sloop Bonetta for New York. At the end of the war he mustered at St. Augustine, Georgia (Florida?) 26 April 1783 where he was part of a group of 329 officers and men under Major James Wright departing for Canada in Fall of 1783 on the ship Nymph and landing at Country Harbour, Guysborough County, Nova Scotia in Dec. 1783.
Source - VNB

LEWIS, W. Henry Esq.
Quarter Master of the 8th. Regiment and widower married again to Elizabeth Colwell on 10 June 1809 by Dr. Stanser found in the Nova Scotia Royal Gazette, Tuesday 13 June 1809 newspaper compiled by Daniel Johnson.
Source - VNB

LINDSAY, Samuel Capt.
Granted with others 8,900 acres 15 Oct. 1784 by Gov. Parr in Kings County, Nova Scotia.
Source - HKC#2

LITTLE, Stephen (Dr.)
Was a physician. New Hampshire General Assembly listed him and 75 others as the enemy in Nov. 1778. Was living at Portsmouth, NH.
Source - NHL

LIVIUS, Peter Esq.
New Hampshire General Assembly listed him and 75 others as the enemy in Nov. 1778. Was living at Portsmouth, NH.
Source - NHL

LOBDELL, Daniel Sr.
From Tryon County, New York near the Mohawk river and was a tenant to Sir John Johnson. Was taken prisoner in April 1780.
Source - HP

LOBDELL, Daniel Jr.
From Tryon County, New York near the Mohawk River and was a tenant to Sir John Johnson. Was taken prisoner in April 1780.
Source - HP

LOBDELL, Isaac
From Tryon County, New York near the Mohawk river and was a tenant of Sir John Johnson. Taken prisoner in April 1780.
Source - HP

LOCKWOOD, Jesse
Listed as Private at Comm. Loyds Neck on muster roll of Capt. Jonathan Randall's company in His Majesty's Loyal American Regiment commanded by Col. Beverly Robinson on 27 August 1778.
Source - DSR2

LONG, David
Listed as Private on muster roll of Capt. John Howard's company of New York Volunteers commanded by Lieut. Col. George Turnbull Esq., Commandant at Paulus Hook, February 1778.
Source - DSR3

LONGEHAFF, William
Listed as Private at Loyds Neck on muster roll of Capt. Jonathan Randall's company in His Majesty's Loyal American Regiment commanded by Col. Beverly Robinson on 27 August 1778.
Source - DSR2

LONGFELLOW, Samuel
From Falmouth, Maine or Massachusetts? Was a mariner and was banished and left the state.
Source - DH

LONGSTREET, John Capt.
Granted with other loyalist refugee's 21,380 acres by Gov. Parr 8 Aug. 1795(85?) in Kings County, Nova Scotia. Excheated 14 May 1814.
Source - HKC#3

LONGYEAR, Andrew
Listed as Private on muster roll of Capt. John Howard's company of New York Volunteers commanded by Lieut. Col. George Turnbull Esq., Commandant at Paulus Hook, February 1778.
Source - DSR3

LORING, Otis
Placed in the Barnstable, Massachusetts (Cape Cod) jail with old man Crocker and a Mr. Davis for being loyalist. While there, they met Seth

Perry (read his section). They later escaped and possibly fled to Newport, Rhode Island, which was British territory.
Source - SA

LOUCKS, George
Listed in Turloch, Tryon County, New York Militia 1775-77 and later in the Kings Royal Rangers of New York.
Source - SJJB

LOUDON, Thomas Lieut.
Granted with other refugee loyalist's 21, 380 acres by Gov. Parr 8 Aug. 1795 (85?) in Kings County, Nova Scotia. Excheated 14 May 1814.
Source - HKC#3

LOVELL, Christopher
From Barnstable, Massachusetts (Cape Cod).
Source - DH

LOVELL, Daniel
From Barnstable, Massachusetts (Cape Cod). His brother was Shubael Lovell.
Source - DH

LOVELL, Shubael
From Barnstable, Massachusetts (Cape Cod).
Was arrested and jailed in 1775 for corresponding with the enemy. His brother was Daniel. He remained after the British left.
Source - DH

LOWE, Zachariah
Listed as Private on muster roll of Capt. John Howard's company of New York Volunteers commanded by Lieut. Col. George Turnbull Esq., Commandant at Paulus Hook, February 1778.
Source - DSR3

LUKER(?), Jacob
Listed as Private on muster roll of Capt. William Gray's company of New York Volunteers from 24 Feb. to 24 April 1781, location unknown.
Source - DSR3

LUTWYCHE, Edward Goldstone Col. Esq.
From Merrimack, New Hampshire and was a member of the Provincial Congress until 1775. Followed Gov. John Wentworth of New Hampshire to Flatbush, Long Island, New York around 1777. New Hampshire General Assembly listed him and 75 others as the enemy in Nov. 1778. On confiscation list of 28 Nov. 1778.
Source - NHL

LYDE, George
Born 1741/2 in Falmouth, Maine or Massachusetts? Was a Customs officer and gentleman. Banished from state in 1777 for Great Britain. His father was Byfield Lyde and Sarah Belcher.
Source - DH

MACDONOUGH, Thomas
Was listed as escorting Gov. John Wentworth of New Hampshire through his exile in Flatbush, Long Island, New York around 1777. He was the Governors secretary.
Source - NHL

MAFIE, Sande
Listed in Turloch, Tryon County, New York Militia 1775-77 and later in the Kings Royal Rangers of New York.
Source - SJJB

MALONE, John
Listed on muster roll of First Battalion of Maryland Loyalist 11 July 1778 at Long Island, New York. Enlisted on 20 Dec. 1777.
Source - ML

MANUEL, Henry Jr.
Listed as a Private in Capt. Peter Ruttan's Company of the 4th. Battalion of the New Jersey Volunteers commanded by Col. Abraham Bushkirk at Staten Island, New York on 18 Nov. 1777. He is listed as taken prisoner on 29 Dec. 1776. He enlisted on 7 Dec. 1776.
Source - DSR

MARCH, Abraham
Listed as loyalist settler in Cornwall, Ontario alone in 1790's.
Source - LCO

MARCLES, Henrick
Listed in Turloch, Tryon County, New York Militia 1775-77 and later in the Kings Royal Rangers of New York.
Source - SJJB

MARCSLES, Severes
Listed in Turloch, Tryon County, New York Militia 1775-77 and later in the Kings Royal Rangers of New York.
Source - SJJB

MARCULES, John
Listed in Turloch, Tryon County, New York Militia 1775-77 and later in the Kings Royal Rangers of New York.
Source - SJJB

MARGSLES, (not clear)
Listed in Turloch, Tryon County, New York Militia 1775-77 and later in the Kings Royal Rangers of New York.
Source - SJJB

MARKLE, Jacob Corporal
From Turloch, Tryon Co., New York. Served in Turloch Militia under Capt. Jacob Miller from 1775-77, then transferred to First Battalion of Kings Royal Rangers of New York. Possibly settled around Williamsburgh, Ontario.
Source - SJJB

MARKS, Edward
Listed as Drummer on muster roll of Capt. Christopher Hatch's Company of Loyal Americans, commanded by Col. Beverly Robinson at Haarlem, New York, possibly at beginning of 1778 and on 21 April 1778 muster.
Source - DSR2

MARR, Lawrence
Listed as Corporal on Muster Roll of Lieut. Col. Stephen Delancey, commanded by Col. Cortland Skinner Esq. dated May 1783 at New Town (location unclear).
Source - DMR

MARTEN, Charles
Listed as Corporal and absent without leave on muster roll of Major Thomas Barclay's company in the Loyal American Regiment commanded by Col. Beverly Robinson at Guanus on 11 May 1782.
Source - DSR2

MARTIN, (?)
Listed as Ensign on muster roll of Major Thomas Barclay's company in the Loyal American Regiment commanded by Col. Beverly Robinson at Guanus on 11 May 1782. There is note saying he was a "prisoner on parole".
Source - DSR2

MARTIN, John
From Falmouth, Maine or Massachusetts? Was a mariner. Property legally labeled for potential confiscation by the state. Left for New York City (British strong hold) in 1781. His Cumberland County, Massachusetts property was forfeited in 1782.
Source - DH

MAY, William
Listed with Sir John Johnston's Brigade and later joined Joseph Brant's Volunteers. Disbanded in 1783 and possibly was granted land in Niagara, Ontario.
Source - SJJB

MABY (see Laby), Peter

MAZE, Benjamin
Listed in Turloch, Tryon County, New York Militia 1775-77 and later in Butler's Rangers.
Source - SJJB

MCALLASTER, Walter
Listed as Private on muster roll of Capt. Christopher Hatch's Company of Loyal Americans, commanded by Col. Beverly Robinson at Haarlem, New York, possibly at beginning of 1778 and on 21 April 1778.
Source - DSR2

MCCLURE, Gilbert
From Falmouth, Maine or Massachusetts? Was a merchant. Property was legally labeled for potential confiscation by the state. He possibly left for

Scotland. Possibly listed in Gen. Skinner's muster roll of Seconded Officers (date unknown).
Source - DH & GSB

MCCOMB, James
Listed on muster roll of First Battalion of Maryland Loyalists 11 July 1778 at Long Island, New York. Enlisted 1 Jan. 1777.
Source - ML

MCDONALD, Alexander Capt.
Granted with others 8,900 acres 15 Oct. 1784 by Gov. Parr in Kings County, Nova Scotia.
Source - HKC#2

MCDONALD, Alexander
Granted 300 acres in Douglas, Nova Scotia for serving in 2nd. Battalion, 84th. Regiment. (not know if same as above Alex). Another granted for 24 acres in Rawdon/Douglas, Nova Scotia under Major General Small.
Source - WWRD

MCDONALD (MCDONGAL), Anne (Widow)
Granted 500 acres in Douglas, Nova Scotia for husband serving in 2nd. Battalion, 84th. Regiment.
Source - WWRD

MCDONALD, Bruce
Listed on grant but not amount noted in Rawdon/Douglas, Nova Scotia under Major General Small.
Source - WWRD

MCDONALD, Donald
Heirs of Donald granted 500 acres and 250 acres at Nine-Mile River, ten miles west of Shubenacadie.
Source - WWRD

MCDONALD, Donald
Granted 300 acres in Douglas, Nova Scotia for serving in 2nd.Battalion, 84th. Regiment. (not sure if same as above).
Source - WWRD

MCDONALD, Donald
Granted 240 acres in Douglas, Nova Scotia for serving in 2nd. Battalion, 84th. Regiment. (not sure if same person as above).
Source - WWRD

MCDONALD (MCDONGAL), Donald
Granted 350 acres in Douglas, Nova Scotia for serving in 2nd. Battalion, 84th. Regiment. (not sure if same person as above Donald's)(another listed as getting 250 acres in same location?)
Source - WWRD

MCDONALD, Duncan
Granted 25 Acres in Five-Mile River, Nova Scotia under Major General Small.
Source - WWRD

MCDONALD, Frances
Listed as Corporal on muster roll of Capt. John Howard's company of New York Volunteers commanded by Lieut. Col. George Turnbull Esq., Commandant at Paulus Hook, February 1778.
Source - DSR3

MCDONALD, John Major
Listed on muster roll of First Battalion of Maryland Loyalists, 11 July 1778 at Long Island, New York. Enlisted 10 Nov. 1777.
Source - ML

MCDONALD, John
Listed with no amount of grant in Rawdon/Douglas, Nova Scotia under Major General Small (possibly one of the below listed John's?) Also listed again for 150 & 400 acres in Five-Mile River, Nova Scotia under Major General Small.
Source - WWRD

MCDONALD, John Jr.
Granted 150 acres in Douglas, Nova Scotia for serving in 2nd. Battalion, 84th. Regiment.
Source - WWRD

MCDONALD, John Sr.
Granted 500 acres in Douglas, Nova Scotia for serving in 2nd. Battalion, 84th. Regiment.

Source - WWRD

MCDONALD, Patrick
Granted 500 acres in Rawdon/Douglas, Nova Scotia under Major General Small.
Source - WWRD

MCDONALD, Peter
Heirs of Peter were granted 100 acres in Rawdon/Douglas, Nova Scotia under Major General Small.
Source - WWRD

MCDONALD, Richard
Listed as Corporal on muster roll of Capt. Christopher Hatch's Company of Loyal Americans, commanded by Col. Beverly Robinson at Haarlem, New York, possibly beginning of 1778 and on 21 April 1778 muster.
Source - DSR2

MCDONEL, John
Listed in Turloch, Tryon County, New York Militia 1775-77 and later in Butler's Rangers.
Source - SJJB

MCDONEL, Peter
Listed in Turloch, Tryon County, New York Militia 1775-77 and later in Butler's Rangers.
Source - SJJB

MCDONOUGH, Thomas Esq.
New Hampshire General Assembly listed him and 75 others as the enemy in Nov. 1778. His home was Portsmouth, NH. On confiscation list of 28 Nov. 1778.
Source - NHL

MCDOUGAL, Donald
Heirs granted 60 acres in Rawdon/Douglas, Nova Scotia under Major General Small.
Source - WWRD

MCELWANE, William
Listed on muster roll of First Battalion of Maryland Loyalists 11 July 1778 at Long Island, New York. Enlisted 8 Dec. 1777. Discharged 30 May 1778.
Source - ML

MCEVOY, Daniel
Listed on muster roll of First Battalion of Maryland Loyalists 11 July 1778 at Long Island, New York. Enlisted 27 Dec. 1777.
Source - ML

MCKENZIE, Donald
Granted 300 acres in Douglas, Nova Scotia for serving in 2nd. Battalion, 84th. Regiment.
Source - WWRD

MCKENZIE, Duncan
Granted 300 acres in Douglas, Nova Scotia for serving in 2nd. Battalion, 84th. Regiment.
Source - WWRD

MCKENZIE, Kennet
Listed as Private on muster roll of Major Thomas Barclay's company in the Loyal American Regiment commanded by Col. Beverly Robinson at Guanus on 11 May 1782.
Source - DSR2

MCLAUREN, Mathew
Granted 500 acres in Rawdon/Douglas, Nova Scotia under Major General Small.
Source - WWRD

MCLEAN, Joseph
Listed as Private on muster roll of Capt. Christopher Hatch's Company of Loyal Americans, commanded by Col. Beverly Robinson at Haarlem, New York, possibly at beginning of 1778 and on 21 April 1778 as sick in quarters.
Source - DSR2

MCLEOD, Donald
Listed as loyalist settler in Cornwall, Ontario in 1790's with 4 dependants.
Source - LCO

MCLOCKLIN, John
Listed in muster roll of First Battalion of Maryland Loyalists 11 July 1778 at Long Island, New York. Enlisted 10 Dec. 1777.
Source - ML

MCMASTERS, James
A Merchant. New Hampshire General Assembly listed him with 75 others as the enemy in Nov. 1778. His home was at Portsmouth, NH. On confiscation list of 28 Nov. 1778.
Source - NHL

MCMASTERS, John
A Merchant. New Hampshire General Assembly listed him and 75 others as the enemy in Nov. 1778. His home was at Portsmouth, NH. On confiscation list of 28 Nov. 1778.
Source - NHL

MCMULLIN, Francois(?)
Listed as a Private in Muster Roll of May 1783 of Lieut. Col. Stephen Delancey, commanded by Col. Cortland Skinner Esq. at New Town (location unclear).
Source - DMR

MCNAMARA(?), Patrick
Listed as Private in May 1783 Muster Roll of Lieut. Col. Stephen Delancey, commanded by Col. Cortland Skinner Esq. at New Town (location unclear).
Source - DMR

MCNEIL, John
Granted 500 acres in Douglas, Nova Scotia for serving in 2nd. Battalion, 84th. Regiment.
Source - WWRD

MCPHEE, Alexander
Granted 300 acres at Nine-Mile River, ten miles west of Shubenacadie, Nova Scotia. Also listed again as getting 500 in Douglas, Nova Scotia for serving in 2nd. Battalion, 84th. Regiment.
Source - WWRD

MCPHEE, Evan

Granted 500 acres in Douglas, Nova Scotia for serving in 2nd. Battalion, 84th. Regiment.
Source - WWRD

MCPHEE, James
Granted 350 acres in Douglas, Nova Scotia for serving in 2nd. Battalion, 84th. Regiment.
Source - WWRD

MCVEAN (MacVain), Colin Sergeant
Listed in 4th. Battalion New Jersey Volunteers muster roll commanded by Lt. Col. Abraham Bushkirk and Capt. Peter Ruton at Staten Island, New York dated March 1778. Also listed as Ensign on 18 Nov. 1777 Muster at same place. Again listed on 6 Jan. 1778 Muster at same place. Again in March and May (on leave at New York) and July and possibly August or September and October and on 30 Dec (recruiting) 1778 Muster at same place.
Source - 4BNJVM & DSR

MEDDOUGH, John
Listed as loyalist settler in Cornwall, Ontario in 1790's with 5 dependants on his land.
Source - LCO

MEDISH, Art
Listed as Private on muster roll of Major Thomas Barclay's company in the Loyal American Regiment commanded by Col. Beverly Robinson at Guanus on 11 May 1782.
Source - DSR2

MENESE (?), John, ...Lieut.
Listed in Gen. Skinner's Brigade muster roll in Seconded Officers (date unknown) at age 29 from Portugal.
Source - GSB

MERKLE, Frederick
Listed in Turloch, Tryon County, New York Militia 1775-77 and later in the Kings Royal Rangers of New York.
Source - SJJB

MERKLE, Hendrick
Listed in Turloch, Tryon County, New York Militia 1775-77 and later in the Kings Royal Rangers of New York.
Source - SJJB

MERKLE, John
Listed in Turloch, Tryon County, New York Militia 1775-77 and later in the Kings Royal Rangers of New York.
Source - SJJB

MESERVE, George Esq.
The Collector of Customs at Portsmouth, New Hampshire. Followed Gov. John Wentworth of New Hampshire to Flatbush, Long Island, New York around 1777. New Hampshire General Assembly listed him and 75 others as the enemy in Nov. 1778. His home was Portsmouth, NH. On confiscation list of 28 Nov. 1778.
Source - NHL

MESSET, Laurence
Listed on muster roll of First Battalion of Maryland Loyalists 11 July 1778 at Long Island, New York. Enlisted 6 Nov. 1777.
Source - ML

MEYERS, Martin
Listed in 4th. Battalion New Jersey Volunteers muster roll commanded by Lt. Col. Abraham Bushkirk and Capt. Peter Ruton at Staten Island, New York dated March 1778. Listed as Private and dead.
Source - 4BNJVM & DSR

MILES, Ambrose
Listed on muster roll of First Battalion of Maryland Loyalist 11 July 1778 at Long Island, New York. Enlisted 18 Dec. 1777.
Source - ML

MILLAGE, Thomas
Late of Morris County, New Jersey, listed Sussex County, NJ 9 Feb. 1779 inquisition at Court of Inquiry with others by Isaac Martin and Samuel Meeker, Commissioners. (could this be the same person as below, Thomas Milledge?).
Source - NJNE

MILLEDGE, Thomas
Was Deputy Surveyor and member of land board of Digby, Nova Scotia 1783-4.
Source - NHL

MILLER, George
Granted 400 acres in Rawdon/Douglas, Nova Scotia under Major General Small.
Source - WWRD

MILLER, Jacob Captain
From Turloch, Tryon Co., New York. Served in Turlock Militia, 1775-77, then transferred to First Battalion, Kings Royal Rangers, of New York. Possibly settled in Williamsburgh, Ontario.
Source - SJJB

MILLER, James Lieut.
Listed on muster roll of First Battalion of Maryland Loyalist on 11 July 1778 at Long Island, New York. Enlisted 26 Oct. 1777.
Source - ML

MILLER, James Adj.
Listed on muster roll of First Battalion of Maryland Loyalists 11 July 1778 at Long Island, New York. Enlisted 26 Oct. 1777.
Source - ML

MITCHEL, George
Listed as loyalist settler in Cornwall, Ontario in 1790's alone.
Source - LCO

MITCHELL, James
Granted with other refugee loyalist's 21, 380 acres by Gov. Parr 8 Aug. 1795 (85?) in Kings County, Nova Scotia.
Source - HKC#3

MITCHELL, John
Listed as Sergeant on muster roll of Capt. John Howard's company of New York Volunteers commanded by Lieut. Col. George Turnbull Esq., Commandant at Paulus Hook, February 1778.
Source - DSR3

The New Loyalist Index 3 105

MIZNER, Henry
Listed in New Jersey Volunteers muster roll commanded by Col. Joseph Barton and Capt. James Shaw dated 4 April 1777.
Source - NJM

MONDWELL, Henery
Listed on Muster Roll of Capt. Peter Ruttan's Company in the 4th. Battalion of New Jersey Volunteers commanded by Lieut. Col. Abraham Bushkirk at Staten Island, New York on 6 Jan. 1778 as a Private who was taken prisoner on 29 Dec. 1776.
Source - DSR

MONROE, John Lieut.
Granted with other refugee loyalist's 21, 380 acres by Gov. Parr 8 Aug. 1795 (85?) in Kings County, Nova Scotia.
Source - HKC#3

MONTONYE, Isaac
Listed in 4th. Battalion New Jersey Volunteers muster roll commanded by Lt. Col. Abraham Bushkirk and Capt. Peter Ruton (Ruttan) at Staten Island, New York March and May 1778. Listed as Private and prisoner of rebels. Also listed on 18 Nov. 1777 Muster at same place as taken prisoner on 29 Dec. 1776 and enlisted on 7 Dec. 1776. Again on 6 Jan. and July and possibly August or September and October and 30 Dec. 1778 Muster at same place and still prisoner. On March 1779 Muster at Hobuck (Hoboken), New Jersey.
Source - 4BNJVM & DSR

MONTONYE (Montonyeh)(Montony), Jacob
Listed as a Private and prisoner with the Rebels on Muster Roll of Capt. Peter Ruttan's Company in the 4th. Battalion of New Jersey Volunteers commanded by Lieut. Col. Abraham Buskirk Esq. (location unknown, but possibly Long Island, New York) in Jan. 1779 and at Powles Hook 7 July 1779 listed as a prisoner with Rebels and again on August 1779 muster and noted that he was taken prisoner before last muster and at Governor's Island on 29 Oct. and Dec. 1779 still prisoner. Also on 19 March and May 1780 muster (location unknown)(prisoner). On 14 July and 11 Sept. and 2 Dec. 1780 muster at Staten Island, New York (prisoner). Listed on 29 April 1781 muster at Staten Island.
Source - DSR

MOON, Augustus
Listed as Private on muster roll of Capt. John Howard's company of New York Volunteers commanded by Lieut. Col. George Turnbull Esq., Commandant at Paulus Hook, February 1778. Again on muster of Capt. William Gray (same company) from 24 Feb. to 24 April 1781, location unknown.
Source - DSR3

MOORE, Thomas
Granted with other refugee loyalist's 21, 380 acres by Gov. Parr 8 Aug. 1795 (85?) in Kings County, Nova Scotia.
Source - HKC#3

MOORE, William
Granted 500 acres at Five-Mile River, Nova Scotia under Major General Small.
Source - WWRD

MORDANT, James
Listed in New Jersey Volunteers muster roll commanded by Col. Joseph Barton and Capt. James Shaw dated 4 Jan. 1777.
Source - NJM

MORGAN, Charles
Listed on muster roll of First Battalion of Maryland Loyalists 11 July 1778 at Long Island, New York. Enlisted 29 Dec. 1777. Listed as sick on board ship.
Source - ML

MORGAN, John
Listed on muster roll of First Battalion of Maryland Loyalists 11 July 1778 at Long Island, New York. Enlisted 11 April 1778.
Source - ML

MORGAN, Reuben
Listed as Private on muster roll of Capt. Christopher Hatch's Company of Loyal Americans, commanded by Col. Beverly Robinson at Haarlem, New York, possibly at beginning of 1778 and on 21 April 1778 muster.
Source - DSR2

MORRIS (Moris)(Mouris), Jacob

Listed in 4th. Battalion New Jersey Volunteers muster roll commanded by Lt. Col. Abraham Bushkirk and Capt. Peter Ruton (Ruttan) at Staten Island, New York dated March and May 1778. Listed as Private and prisoner of the rebels. Also listed on 18 Nov. 1777 Muster at same place as prisoner on 29 Dec. 1776 and enlisted on 7 Dec. 1776. Again on 6 Jan. and July and possibly August or September and October 1778 Muster at same place and still prisoner.
Source - 4BNJVM & DSR

MORRIS, John
Listed in Gen. Skinner's Brigade muster roll with Seconded Officers (date unknown). He was
from America, age 48.
Source - GSB

MORRIS, Robert Capt.
Listed in Gen. Skinner's Brigade muster roll of Seconded Officers (date unknown).
Source - GSB

MORRISON, Allen
Listed on muster roll of First Battalion of Maryland Loyalists 11 July 1778 at Long Island, New York. Enlisted 23 Dec. 1777, and on duty.
Source - ML

MORRISON, John
A clerk from Peterborough, NH (not sure if the same person as listed below) The New Hampshire General Assembly listed him and 75 others as the enemy in Nov. 1778.
Source - NHL

MORRISON, John
Was from New Hampshire and became attached to the Commissary Department of the King's forces after the battle of Bunker Hill.
Source - NHL

MORRISON (MORISON)(?), Thomas Lieut.
Listed in Gen. Skinner's Brigade muster roll, Seconded Officers (date unknown) at age 39 from England.
Source - GSB

MORY, James
Listed as Private in General Hospital on muster roll of Capt. William Gray's company of New York Volunteers from 24 Feb. to 24 April 1781, location unknown.
Source - DSR3

MOSHER, Joseph
Granted 550 acres in Five-Mile River, Nova Scotia under Major General Small.
Source - WWRD

MOSURE, Stephen
Listed as Private on muster roll of Capt. John Howard's company of New York Volunteers commanded by Lieut. Col. George Turnbull Esq., Commandant at Paulus Hook, February 1778. Again on muster of Capt. William Gray (same company) from 24 Feb. to 24 April 1781, location unknown.
Source - DSR3

MOTT, Jacob
Listed as Private on muster roll of Capt. John Howard's company of New York Volunteers commanded by Lieut. Col. George Turnbull Esq., Commandant at Paulus Hook, February 1778. Again on muster of Capt. William Gray (same company) from 24 Feb. to 24 April 1781, location unknown.
Source - DSR3

MOTTS, Richard
Listed as Corporal on muster roll of Capt. William Gray's company of New York Volunteers from 24 Feb. to 24 April 1781, location unknown.
Source - DSR3

MULLIN, Patrick
Listed as Private on muster roll of Major Thomas Barclay's company in the Loyal American Regiment commanded by Col. Beverly Robinson at Guanus on 11 May 1782.
Source - DSR2

MUNRO, John Lieut.
Listed in Gen. Skinner's Brigade muster roll in Seconded Officers (date unknown) at age 23 from America. (possibly same person as above John Monroe?)

Source - GSB

MURDOCK, Findley (Findlay)
Granted 500 acres in Douglas, Nova Scotia for possibly serving in 2nd. Battalion, 84th. Regiment. Listed again as getting 500 acres in Rawdon/Douglas, NS under Major General Small.
Source - WWRD

MURPHY, John
Listed as Private on muster roll of Capt. John Howard's company of New York Volunteers commanded by Lieut. Col. George Turnbull Esq., Commandant at Paulus Hook, February 1778. Again on muster of Capt. William Gray (same company) from 24 Feb. to 24 April 1781, location unknown.
Source - DSR3

MURRAY, Daniel Capt.
Listed on muster roll of Corps of loyalists Volunteers associated with Gov. John Wentworth previous of New Hampshire now located at Flushing, Long Island, New York 16 Oct. 1777. He was from Rutland, Massachusetts.
Source - NHL

MYERS, Martin
Listed on Muster Roll of Capt. Peter Ryttan's Company in the 4th. Battalion of the New Jersey Volunteers commanded by Col. Abraham Bushkirk at Staten Island, New York as a Private and deceased on 20 July 1777. He enlisted on 7 Dec. 1776.
Source - DSR

NADON(?), Bartholomew
Listed as Private and confined with Rebels on muster roll of Major Thomas Barclay's company in the Loyal American Regiment commanded by Col. Beverly Robinson at Guanus on 11 May 1782.
Source - DSR2

NASH, Joseph
Listed as a Private on Muster Roll of Capt. Peter Rutton's Company in the 4th. Battalion of New Jersey Volunteers commanded by Lieut. Col. Abraham Buskirk at Powles Hook 7 July 1779. Listed again on August 1779 muster in same company and at Governor's Island on 29 Oct. 1779 and Dec. 1779.

Source - DSR

NEIL, Joseph
Listed as Private in May 1783 Muster Roll of Lieut. Col. Stephen Delancey, commanded by Col. Cortland Skinner Esq. at New Town (location unclear).
Source - DMR

NELSON, Annenias
Listed on muster roll of First Battalion of Maryland Loyalists 11 July 1778 at Long Island, New York. Enlisted on 27 March 1778.
Source - ML

NELSON, John
Listed as Private on muster roll of Capt. John Howard's company of New York Volunteers commanded by Lieut. Col. George Turnbull Esq., Commandant at Paulus Hook, February 1778. Listed again on muster of Capt. William Gray (same company) from 24 Feb. to 24 April 1781, location unknown.
Source - DSR3

NELSON, John
Listed as Private (two John Nelson's listed) on muster roll of Capt. William Gray's company of New York Volunteers from 24 Feb. to 24 April 1781, location unknown.
Source - DSR3

NELSON, John
Listed as Private at Comm. Loyds Neck on muster roll of Capt. Jonathan Randall's company in His Majesty's Loyal American Regiment commanded by Col. Beverly Robinson on 27 August 1778.
Source - DSR2

NELSON, William
Listed as Sergeant with Col. Innes on muster roll of Capt. Jonathan Randall's company in His Majesty's Loyal American Regiment commanded by Col. Beverly Robinson on 27 August 1778.
Source - DSR2

NEWCOMB, William
Was said to take part in the attack on Dr. Freeman in Sandwich, Barnstable Co., Massachusetts (Cape Cod), but stayed behind after the war.
Source - SA

NEW HOUSEN, Bortus (Barthus)
Listed as a Private on Muster Roll of Capt. Peter Ruttan's Company in the 4th. Battalion of New Jersey Volunteers commanded by Lieut. Col. Abraham Buskirk Esq. (place not give) in Jan. 1779. Also on 19 March and May 1780 muster (location unknown). On 14 July and 11 Sept. and 2 Dec. 1780 muster at Staten Island, New York. Listed on 29 April 1781 muster at Staten Island.
Source - DSR

NEWMAN, Arthur
Listed on land grant petition 12 July 1793 to John Graves Simcoe, Esq. for land located between Long Point and Turkey Point on the west side of Lake Erie.
Source - EGRS

NEWMAN, Joseph
From Tryon County, New York, near the Mohawk River and was a tenant to Col. Claus. Taken prisoner in April 1780.
Source - HP

NICHOLSON, Arthur Cornet
Became the commander of the garrison at Presquisle, New Brunswick.
Source - NHL

NICKERSON, Annice
Daughter of Nathaniel and Annice (Selleck) Nickerson, born 14 Dec. 1766 possibly in Danbury, Connecticut or New York married Eliakam Andrews 28 Sept. 1785/6. (descends from Cape Cod Nickerson's)
Source - NF

NICKERSON, Chloe
Daughter of Nathaniel and Annice (Selleck) Nickerson, born 2 May 1762 possibly Danbury, Connecticut or New York. Had to relocated with family as loyalist to New Brunswick, Canada in 1783. Descends from Cape Cod Nickerson.
Source - NF

NICKERSON, Elihu
Daughter of Nathaniel and Annice (Selleck) Nickerson, born 19 May 1764 possibly in Danbury, Connecticut or New York. Married a Mr. Gitty. Descends from Cape Cod Nickerson's.
Source - NF

NICKERSON, Eliud
Son of Nathaniel and Annice (Selleck) Nickerson, born Dec. 1760 Danbury, Fairfield County, Connecticut. Married c. 1784 (1) Mary Margaret Frizt (Lutz?) and died 22 March 1840 age 75 at St. Catherines, Ontario. and he married again after 1840 (2) to Hannah Haly, widow of Robert Conn.. He died 30 March 1843 age 75 at St. Catherines, Grantham Township, Lincoln County, Ontario, Canada. Buried at Hodgkinson Burying Grown, SW corner of lot 10, conc. 2 and was moved because of the building of the 4th. Welland Canal (see 1876 Hist. Atlas). Eliud was a very active loyalist who later went to New Brunswick in 1783. He was tried on 13 Oct. 1801 by Home District, Upper Canada at York (now Toronto) court for various felonies and trespassing charges along with 11 others. Was the first inhabitant of Cobourg living in a crude log hut near present day King Davidson section in 1798, receiving lot # 16 in 1802. Out of several children he had Nathaniel, John, Eliud, Levi, Mary, Enos, Eunice, David and Catherine. Descends from Cape Cod Nickerson's.
Source - NF

NICKERSON, Ephraim
Son of Nathaniel and Annice (Selleck) Nickerson, born 2 Nov. 1771 possibly New York and died after 1819. Possibly lived in Cobourg, Ontario in 1804 near Eliud Nickerson, had 6 in family on 1804 census there. By 1815, the family grew too 11, 3 sons and 6 daughters. Descends from Cape Cod Nickerson's.
Source - NF

NICKERSON, Joseph
Son of Nathaniel and Hannah (Hamblin) Nickerson of Chatham, Barnstable County, Massachusetts (Cape Cod). Born around 1750 possibly in Danbury, Connecticut, but later possibly moved to Oblong, Putnam County and Croton, Dutchess County, New York. Died at Gagetown, Queens County, New Brunswick, Canada before 4 March 1796 (when his will was proved). Was listed as a Loyalist Refugee in Unit S who sailed for Saint John, New Brunswick in 1783 after the war from New York. He was listed as a Pennsylvania loyalist. He married (1) to Martha Noble, daughter of Gideon Noble and Martha Prime, born 16 Aug. 1752 at New

Milford, Connecticut. He married (2) again to Sarah (possibly Barton), daughter of Roger Barton. Joseph was in prison in the Poughkeepsie Goal and escaped Feb. 1780. Had one child by first wife Martha, named Almeida possibly born in New York. Child from 2nd. marriage was George.
Source - NF

NICKERSON, Lucy
Daughter of Nathaniel and Annice (Selleck) Nickerson, born Danbury, Fairfield County, Connecticut 25 Aug. 1776. Descends from Cape Cod Nickerson's.
Source - NF

NICKERSON, Nathaniel
Son of Nathaniel and Hannah (Hamblin) Nickerson of Chatham, Barnstable County, Massachusetts (Cape Cod). Born 10 Oct. 1732 (a twin to brother, Nathan) at possibly Danbury, Connecticut and relocated to Oblong, Putnam County, and Croton River, Dutchess County, New York. He married Annice Selleck possibly at Fairfield County, Connecticut around 1759. Served as soldier in Col. Delancy's 2nd. Battalion from New York. He died in 1783 in Nova Scotia, which is now New Brunswick. He son was Eliud Nickerson, also a loyalist. Other children were; Chloe, Elihu, Annice, Rebecca, Ephraim and Lucy.
Source - NF

NICKERSON, Rebecca
Daughter of Nathaniel and Annice (Selleck) Nickerson, born 24 March 1768 possibly in New York married Abraham Wildman 15 Oct. 1791. Descends from Cape Cod Nickerson's.
Source - NF

NICKERSON, Thomas
Son of Nathaniel and Hannah (Hamblin) Nickerson of Chatham, Barnstable County, Massachusetts (Cape Cod). Born possibly in Danbury, Connecticut and relocated to Oblong, Putnam County and Croton River, Dutchess County, New York. Died after 1796 at Hempsted, New Brunswick, Canada. Was listed in Loyalist Refugee Unit S who sail on the ship, Hope in 1783 for Saint John, New Brunswick after the war along with his family, brother Joseph and nephew Eliud. He was listed as a Pennsylvania loyalist.
Source - NF

NIX (Niex), Christopher
Listed in 4th. Battalion New Jersey Volunteers muster roll commanded by Lt. Col. Abraham Bushkirk and Capt. Peter Ruton (Ruttan) at Staten Island, New York dated March 1778. Listed as Private and dead. Also listed on 18 Nov. 1777 at same place as sick in the Regiment Hospital. He enlisted on 22 Jan. 1777. Again listed on 6 Jan. 1778 Muster at same place and deceased on 5 Jan. 1778.
Source - 4BNJVM & DSR

NIX, Peter
Listed in 4th. Battalion New Jersey Volunteers muster roll commanded by Lt. Col. Abraham Bushkirk and Capt. Peter Ruton (Ruttan) at Staten Island, New York dated March 1778. Listed as Private and dead. Also listed on 18 Nov. 1777 Muster at same place as deceased on 10 July 1777. Enlisted on 22 Jan. 1777.
Source - 4BNJVM & DSR

NORTHREY, Azer
Listed with Sir John Johnston's Brigade and later joined Joseph Brant's Volunteers. Disbanded in 1783 and possibly granted land in Niagara, Ontario.
Source - SJJB

NOWLAN, John Quartermaster
Granted with other loyalist refugee's 21,380 acres by Gov. Parr 8 Aug. 1795(85?) in Kings County, Nova Scotia.
Source - HKC#3

NYBERG, William
Listed in Turloch, Tryon County, New York Militia 1775-77 and later in the Kings Royal Rangers of New York.
Source - SJJB

OCKERMAN, Abraham
Listed in Muster Roll of Capt. Peter Ruttan's Company in the 4th. Battalion of New Jersey Volunteers commanded by Lieut. Col. Abraham Bushkirk at Staten Island, New York on 6 Jan. 1778 as a Private.
Source - DSR

ODEL, Jonathan
Listed as Private on muster roll of Capt. Christopher Hatch's Company of Loyal Americans, commanded by Col. Beverly Robinson at Haarlem, New York, possibly at beginning of 1778 and on 21 April 1778.
Source - DSR2

O'HALA, Dennis
A yeoman from Londonderry, NH. The New Hampshire General Assembly listed him with 75 others as the enemy in Nov. 1778.
Source - NHL

ORSEN, Eisack
Listed in Turloch, Tryon County, New York Militia 1775-77 and later in the Kings Royal Rangers of New York.
Source - SJJB

ORSEN, John
Listed in Turloch, Tryon County, New York Militia 1775-77 and later in the Kings Royal Rangers of New York.
Source - SJJB

ORTHOUSE(?), Israel
Listed as Private at Comm. Loyds Neck on muster roll of Capt. Jonathan Randall's company in His Majesty's Loyal American Regiment commanded by Col. Beverly Robinson on 24 August 1778.
Source - DSR2

OSBURN, ...?
Listed as Private on muster roll of Capt. William Gray's company of New York Volunteers from 24 Feb. to 24 April 1781, location unknown.
Source - DSR3

OTMAN, Henrick
Listed in Turloch, Tryon County, New York Militia 1775-77 and later in the Kings Royal Rangers of New York.
Source - SJJB

PACKER, Connrate H.
Listed as a Private on 18 Nov. 1777 Muster Roll at Staten Island, New York as on command as a Taylor. He enlisted on 22 Jan. 1777.
Source - DSR

PACKER, Philip H.
Listed as a Private on 18 Nov. 1777 Muster Roll at Staten Island, New York stating that he enlisted on 22 Jan. 1777.
Source - DSR

PADDOCK, Adino Colonel
Born 14 March 1727 and was baptized 31 March 1728 at the First Church in Harwich, Barnstable County, Massachusetts (Cape Cod). Son of John Paddock and Rebecca Thatcher their roots go back to Robert Paddock who was one of the Pilgrims in Plymouth, Massachusetts. After his father, John died in 1732, the family removed to Boston where he married Lydia Snelling, daughter of Robert Snelling and Lydia Dexter. He became a coach maker and was famous. A story of some famous elm trees outside his shop is told in detail in the source materials. Adino became Captain of the train of artillery in Boston in 1774. This gun house was located at the corner of West and Tremont streets. When mobs started, Adino expressed his intention to turn the gun house over to General Gage for safekeeping. He belonged to the Loyalist Party, but had to leave Boston during the evacuation of 17 March 1776. There was nine in the family going to Halifax, Nova Scotia, but the following June he left with his wife and children for England. In 1778 he was officially banished and from 1781 until his death he lived on the Isle of Jersey where he held office of Inspector of Artillery Stores with a rank of Captain. As Colonel he received a partial compensation for his losses as a loyalist. He died 25 March 1804 at the age of 76. His wife Lydia died there in 1781 at age 51. Colonel Paddock's house in Boston was located at the south corner of Bromfield and Tremont streets, formerly Common Street and Ransom Lane. He and his wife had a total of 13 children with 9 dying in infancy and a John Paddock who was a student at Harvard drowned while bathing in the Charles River in 1773. His son Adino finally ending up settling in New Brunswick, Canada where he lived out his life.
Source - LMTOS

PADDOCK, Adino (Surgeon)
Son of Adino Paddock of Massachusetts. Listed as going to New Brunswick possibly 1783 or after and became a well-known physician there.
Source - NHL

PAGE, John
Listed on Muster Roll of Capt. Peter Ruton's Company in the 4th. Battalion of New Jersey Volunteers commanded by Lieut. Col. Abraham

Buskirk (Bushkirk) at Staten Island, New York in possibly August or September, October and 30 Dec. 1778. He enlisted on 27 July 1778. Listed again on Muster dated Jan. 1779 (place unknown). On March 1779 Muster at Hobuck (Hoboken), New Jersey and at Powles Hook 7 July 1779 and again on August 1779 muster but listed as taken prisoner on 19 Aug. 1779 and at Governor's Island on 29 Oct. and Dec. 1779 still prisoner. Also on 19 March and May 1780 muster (location unknown) saying he "joined the Battalion again and in regiment hospital". On 14 July and 11 Sept. and 2 Dec. (sick in regiment hospital) 1780 muster at Staten Island, New York.
Source - DSR

PAGE, Thomas
Listed on muster roll of First Battalion of Maryland Loyalists 11 July 1778 at Long Island, New York. Enlisted 26 Oct. 1777. Deserted 30 June 1778.
Source - ML

PARR, Harriet
Granted with others 2,800 acres, lot #60, 700 acres in Parrsborough, Nova Scotia 8 Aug. 1795(85?).
Source - HKC#1

PARR, John Jr.
Granted with others 2,800 acres, lot #58, 700 acres in Parrsborough, Nova Scotia 8 Aug. 1795(85?).
Source - HKC#1

PARR, Thomas Esq.
Granted with others 2,800 acres 8 Aug. 1795(85?), lot #57, 700 acres in Parrsborough, Nova Scotia.
Source - HKC#1

PARR, William
Granted with others 2,800 acres, lot #59, 700 acres in Parrsborough, Nova Scotia 8 Aug. 1795(85?).
Source - HKC#1

PARRY, Edward Esq.
New Hampshire General Assembly listed him and 75 others as the enemy in Nov. 1778. His home was Portsmouth, NH.
Source - NHL

PATTERSON, Conrad Sergeant
Listed as loyalist settler/Sergeant in Cornwall, Ontario in 1790's alone.
Source - LCO

PATTERSON (Paterson), John Chaplin
Listed on muster roll of First Battalion of Maryland Loyalists 11 July 1778 at Long Island, New York.
Source - ML

PERRY, Alenson
Child of Thomas and Sarah Perry of Sandwich, Barnstable County, Massachusetts (Cape Cod). Left that town as loyalist's refugees, but returned once to visit family. Mother possibly died before 1782. Listed with mother on petition to Massachusetts House of Representetives 17 June 1778 to let them live with father in exile which was granted 14 Dec. 1778.
Source - SA

PERRY, Anne
Daughter of Seth and Lydia Perry of Sandwich, Barnstable County, Massachusetts (Cape Cod). Mother petitioned the Massachusetts House of Representatives on 17 June 1778 to join her husband in exile. It was finally granted on 14 Dec. 1778.
Source - SA

PERRY, Betty
Daughter of Samuel and Thankful Perry of Sandwich, Barnstable County, Massachusetts (Cape Cod). Mother petitioned the Massachusetts House of Representatives on 17 June 1778 to join her husband in exile with Betty and other children. First ignored, then finally granted on 14 Dec. 1778.
Source - SA

PERRY, Edward
Son of Samuel and Thankful Perry from Sandwich, Barnstable County, Massachusetts (Cape Cod). On 17 June 1778 mother petitioned the Massachusetts House of representatives to join her husband listing Edward and other children. This was first ignored, then granted on 14 Dec. 1778.
Source - SA

PERRY, Edward
Listed as loyalist settler in Cornwall, Ontario in 1790's alone.
Source - LCO

PERRY, Experience
She was the second wife of Thomas Perry who was from Sandwich, Massachusetts (Cape Cod). They married in 1782 possibly at Long Island, New York. The first wife of Thomas was Sarah (Blackwell) (possible relation?). The estate in Sandwich was confiscated.
Source - SA

PERRY, John
Listed in Turloch, Tryon County, New York Militia 1775-77 and later in the Kings Royal Rangers of New York.
Source - SJJB

PERRY, Lydia
Wife of Seth Perry who were banished from Sandwich, Massachusetts (Cape Cod) and fled to Long Island, New York as loyalist refugee's. She was allowed a visit back to Sandwich, but returned for good by 1790. She petitioned the Massachusetts House of Representatives on 17 June 1778 with her children Nathan and Anne to join her husband in exile. It was finally granted on 14 Dec. 1778.
Source - SA

PERRY, Martha
Wife of Stephen Perry, she stayed in Sandwich, Massachusetts (Cape Cod) probably because by 1783 she is listed as a widow. The town was thinking of selling the estate, but would have Martha as a Town charge (TM3 p.121) in 1783.

PERRY, Nathan
Son of Seth and Lydia Perry of Sandwich, Barnstable County, Massachusetts (Cape Cod). Mother petitioned the Massachusetts House of Representatives on 17 June 1778 to join her husband in exile. It was finally granted on 14 Dec. 1778.
Source - SA

PERRY, Rufus
Son of Samuel and Thankful Perry from Sandwich, Barnstable County, Massachusetts (Cape Cod). Mother petitioned the Massachusetts House of Representatives on 17 June 1778 to join her husband in exile with Rufus

and other children. First ignored, they granted her second plea on 14 Dec. 1778.
Source - SA

PERRY, Samuel
From Sandwich, Barnstable County, Massachusetts (Cape Cod). Was a mariner and Yeoman. He owned a house and 100 acres. Family property legally labeled for potential confiscation by the state. He was banished and left with his family in 1777 for Shelburne, Nova Scotia. Before that he fled to Rhode Island as a refugee in Sept. 1777 till the end of the war (AO.13/93). His wife Thankful visited Sandwich while they were loyalist refugee's living on Long Island before 1783.
Source - DH & LMTOS & LMTMPC & SA

PERRY, Samuel Jr.
From Sandwich, Barnstable County, Massachusetts (Cape Cod). Was banished and left as father did in 1777.
Source - DH

PERRY, Sarah
She was the first wife of Thomas Perry from Sandwich, Massachusetts (Cape Cod). Their children visited Sandwich from Long Island, New York and before 1782 Sarah must have died or left Thomas because he remarries Experience Blackwell in 1782 (possibly relation?). The estate in Sandwich was confiscated. Children were: Alenson, Thomas and Sarah. She petitioned the Massachusetts House of Representetives to let them join her husband in exile on 17 June 1778 which was finally granted 14 Dec. 1778.
Source - SA

PERRY, Sarah
Daughter to Thomas and Sarah Perry of Sandwich, Barnstable County, Massachusetts (Cape Cod). Left town as loyalist refugee's to Long Island, New York, but returned to visit family. Mother died possibly before 1782. Listed on mothers petition to Massachusetts House of Representetives 17 June 1778 to let them join her husband and father, Thomas Perry in exile which was granted 14 Dec. 1778.
Source - SA

PERRY, Seth
Was labeled as a loyalist and was banished from Sandwich, Massachusetts (Cape Cod), but returned by 1790. Wife was Lydia and they lived on Long

Island, New York as loyalist refugees. Before 30 March 1778 Seth, a mariner, was on board his ship (sloop) possibly anchored in Barnstable Harbor. He was told to come ashore to take the oath of allegiance by a Mr. Pope. His two mates, Mr. Raymond and Cobb told him not to go and to sail for Newport, Rhode Island right away which was still in British hands. He went ashore anyway, but upon arriving, Mr. Pope advised him that they had a warrant for his arrest. Claiming to have taken the oath, he was still placed in the Barnstable jail. Raymond and Cobb took the ship to British territory. Meeting Otis Loring, old man Mr. Crocker and a Mr. Davis in jail he was present with an escape plot which Raymond and Cobb were part of. The Patriots thought Seth was part of it. The escape was made by all with others, but Seth stayed behind, but was still held for possession of counterfeit bills that were smuggled from Newport and found in his house. Judge Nathaniel Freeman, M.D. and Colonel of the Militia and Seth Freeman tried the case along with Seth's wife Lydia, his sister-in-law Sarah who was the wife of Thomas Perry, his brother. Bills were found in Raymond's desk and Seth claims that he burnt the ones he found in his house. He was sentenced to 40 days for failure to report to Ensign Ellis, but was never released so he escaped to Newport where he supported himself by supplying firewood to that settlement. It was found later that the Tory underground met at Seth's house while the counterfeit bills were there (Paper on loyalists by Henry J. Perry, 29 April 1985). Others who met at his house and who were part of the Tory underground were: Ammi Chase, Lemuel Vourne, John Blackwell Jr., Silas Perry, Thomas Bumpus, William Bourne, Caleb Wheaten, Thomas Perry, Frances Trying, Ephraim Ellis Jr., Nicolas Cobb, Joshua Wellbore, Stephen Perry, Nehamiah Webb, Elisha Bourne and Edward Bourne. He had two children; Nathan and Anne. Seth wrote his enemy, Brigadier Freeman to thank him for the release of his wife, which he wrote on 20 Dec. 1778 from Newport, Rhode Island. He did criticized him for falsely spreading rumors about him and that he was trying to go to France. Seth says that he is an American, was born and brought up under the great protector of Protestant Faith, Great Britain, he has no love for France or its Christian King or any of popish superstitions regardless of what the Brigadier or Raymond says with his evil tongue. He petitioned the Massachusetts Governor for restoration of his American citizenship and stop the sale of his mother's house which he was the heir, making it Tory property. He did succeed.
Source - SA

PERRY, Silas
From Sandwich, Barnstable County, Massachusetts (Cape Cod). Was a laborer. Sought refuge in Rhode Island in March of 1778 with Stephen Perry. He went to Nova Scotia. He was found to be part of a Tory underground on Cape Cod.
Source - LMTMPC & SA

PERRY, (Squaw - Native American)
Listed as a "squaw maid" in a petition to the Massachusetts House of Representatives on 17 June 1778 by Thankful Perry to join her loyalist husband Samuel Perry in exile. This release was finally granted on 14 Dec. 1778. This woman was probably Wampanoag because of her home location in Sandwich, Barnstable County, Massachusetts (Cape Cod). I list her only because she too had loses of her family and life on Cape Cod because of her association with the Perry family.

PERRY, Stephen
From Sandwich, Barnstable County, Massachusetts (Cape Cod). Was a laborer. Sought refuge in Rhode Island in March of 1778. He was banished. His wife Martha stayed behind probably because by 1783 she is listed as a widow. The town thought of selling the estate, but would then have Martha as a Town charge (TM3 p.121) in 1783. Was part of the Tory underground and met at Seth Perry's house (see his listing) with other loyalists.
Source - LMTOS & LMTMPC & SA

PERRY, Thankful
Wife of Samuel Perry who was banished from Sandwich, Massachusetts (Cape Cod) for being a loyalist. She revisited Sandwich from Long Island, New York before 1783. She petitioned the Massachusetts House of Representatives to join her husband on 17 June 1778, which was ignored, but later granted on 14 Dec. 1778. This included their children; Edward, Thomas, Rufus, Betty, William and a squaw maid.
Source - SA

PERRY, Thomas
Son of Samuel and Thankful Perry of Sandwich, Barnstable County, Massachusetts (Cape Cod). Mother petitioned the Massachusetts House of Representatives on 17 June 1778 to join her husband in exile listing Thomas and other children. First ignored, this was finally granted on 14 Dec. 1778.
Source - SA

PERRY, Thomas
From Sandwich, Barnstable County, Massachusetts (Cape Cod). Was a Yeoman. Took bounty offer to commission the construction of a new 65-ton coastal schooner at Shelburne, Nova Scotia. His partnership included William and John Roxby, loyalists Thomas Bingay Jr. of Massachusetts and Johannis (John) Ackermann of Bergen County, New Jersey. This was shortly after 14 September 1797. He was banished and settled in Nova Scotia. His estate was confiscated. Children from his former wife, Sarah (Blackwell) visited Sandwich from Long Island, New York probably before 1783. In 1782 Thomas married Experience Blackwell and went to Nova Scotia probably in 1783 when the loyalist left New York for Canada. He was part of a Tory underground on Cape Cod and was at Seth Perry's house (see his listing) for a loyalist meeting.
Source - DLR & LMTOS & SA

PERRY, Thomas
Son of Thomas and Sarah Perry of Sandwich, Barnstable County, Massachusetts (Cape Cod). Left that town as loyalist's refugee's for Long Island, New York. Returned to visit family member, but mother possibly died before 1782. Listed on mothers petition to Massachusetts House of Representetives 17 June 1778 to let them live with husband and father Thomas Perry in exile which was finally granted 14 Dec. 1778.
Source - SA

PERRY, William
Son of Samuel and Thankful Perry from Sandwich, Barnstable County, Massachusetts (Cape Cod). Mother petitioned the Massachusetts House of Representatives on 17 June 1778 to join her husband in exile along with William and other children. First ignored, they granted her wish on 14 Dec. 1778.
Source - SA

PERSON, John
Listed on land grant petition 12 July 1793 to John Graves Simcoe, Esq. for land located between Long Point and Turkey Point on the west side of Lake Erie.
Source - EGRS

PEVEY, William
A Mariner. New Hampshire General Assembly listed him and 75 others as the enemy in Nov. 1778. His home was at Portsmouth, NH.
Source - NHL

PHINNEY, Francis
From Sandwich, Barnstable County, Massachusetts (Cape Cod). Was a Yeoman. Family property was taken. Was cited by town or committee of correspondence for being a Tory in 1778. Barnstable property forfeited and confiscated in 1781. Family left in 1777.
Source - DH & SA

PICKERT, Barthlow
From Tyron County, New York near the Mohawk river and was a tenant of Col. Claus. Taken prisoner in April 1780.
Source - HP

PIERCE, John
The House of Representatives on 13 June 1777 granted him permission to leave Portsmouth, New Hampshire where he was in prison to go to Britain or to the West Indies and to never return to the continent again.
Source - NHL

PITCHER, William
Listed as a Drummer in May 1783 Muster Roll of Lieut. Col. Stephen Delancey, commanded by Col. Cortland Skinner Esq. at New Town (location unclear).
Source - DMR

PLAINFORTH, George Capt.
Listed in Gen. Skinner's muster roll of Seconded Officers (date unknown).
Source - GSB

PLATO, Christian
Listed with Sir John Johnston's Brigade and later joined Joseph Brant's Volunteers. Disbanded in 1783 and possibly granted land in Niagara, Ontario.
Source - SJJB

PLAYS, John Emmerick
Listed with Sir John Johnston's Brigade and later joined Joseph Brant's Volunteers. Disbanded in 1783 and possibly granted land in Niagara, Ontario.
Source - SJJB

PLUMB, Caleb
Listed as Private on muster roll of Capt. Jonathan Randall's company in His Majesty's Loyal American Regiment commanded by Col. Beverly Robinson on 27 August 1778 (location unknown).
Source - DSR2

POMPOY (Pomroy), Josiah (Dr.)
A physician from Keene, NH. The New Hampshire General Assembly listed him and 75 others as the enemy in Nov. 1778. On confiscation list as Pomroy on 28 Nov. 1778.
Source - NHL

PORTER, John
Sergeant in Muster Roll of May 1783 of Lieut. Col. Stephen Delancey, commanded by Col. Cortland Skinner Esq. at New Town (location unclear).
Source - DMR

POTTINSON, Thomas
Granted land 15 Oct. 1784 by Gov. Parr with others in 8.900 acres.
Source - HKC#2

POTTS, Abraham
Listed as Private and confined with Rebels on muster roll of Major Thomas Barclay's company in the Loyal American Regiment commanded by Col. Beverly Robinson at Guanus on 11 May 1782.
Source - DSR2

POWEL, John
Listed on muster roll of First Battalion of Maryland 11 July 1778 at Long Island, New York. Enlisted on 13 Nov. 1777.
Source - ML

PRENTIS, Daniel
Listed as loyalist settler in Cornwall, Ontario in 1790's with 6 dependants.
Source - LCO

PRICKMAN, Rhinehard (Rynard)
Listed in 4th. Battalion New Jersey Volunteers muster roll commanded by Lt. Col. Abraham Bushkirk and Capt. Peter Ruton (Ruttan) at Staten Island, New York dated March 1778. Listed as Private and dead. Also

listed on 18 Nov. 1777 Muster at same place as a Corporal who enlisted on 7 Dec. 1776.
Source - 4BNJVM & DSR

PRIOR (Pryor), Joseph
Listed as a Drummer in Capt. Peter Ruton's Company in the 4th. Battalion of New Jersey Volunteers commanded by Lieut. Col. Abraham Buskirk (Bushkirk) at Staten Island in May and July and possibly August or September and October (Sick in quarters) 1778. Listed again on 30 Dec. 1778 Muster at same place. On March 1779 Muster at Hobuck (Hoboken), New Jersey.
Source - DSR

PRITCHARD, Thomas J. Lieut.
Granted with others 8,900 acres 15 Oct. 1784 by Gov. Parr in Kings County, Nova Scotia. Also listed in Gen. Skinner's Brigade muster roll, Seconded Officers (date unknown) at age 47 from England.
Source - HKC#2 & GSB

PRITCHET(?), John
Listed as Private in May 1783 Muster Roll of Lieut. Col. Stephen Delancey, commanded by Col. Cortland Skinner Esq. at New Town (location unclear).
Source - DMR

PULLIS, Christian
Listed in 4th. Battalion New Jersey Volunteers muster roll commanded by Lt. Col. Abraham Bushkirk and Capt. Peter Ruton at Staten Island, New York dated March 1778. Listed as Private and discharged.
Source - 4BNJVM & DSR

QUIGLEY, John Esq.
From Francestown, NH. The New Hampshire General Assembly listed him and 75 others as the enemy in Nov. 1778. On confiscation list of 28 Nov. 1778.
Source - NHL

RADIG, John
Listed in Turloch, Tryon County, New York Militia 1775-77 and later in the Kings Royal Rangers of New York.
Source - SJJB

RAFTER, John
Granted 250 acres in Douglas, Nova Scotia for possibly serving in 2nd. Battalion, 84th. Regiment.
Source - WWRD

RAMBOUG, Jacob
Listed as loyalist settler in Cornwall, Ontario in 1790's with 5 dependants.
Source - LCO

RAMSEY, Peter
Listed in 4th. Battalion New Jersey Volunteers muster roll commanded by Lt. Col. Abraham Bushkirk and Capt. Peter Ruton (Ruttan) at Staten Island, New York dated March 1778. Listed as Corporal. Also listed on 18 Nov. 1777 Muster at same place. He enlisted on 7 Dec. 1776. Again on 6 Jan. 1778 Muster at same place. Again on March, May, July (sick) and possibly August or September 1778 Muster at same place and sick on Staten Island. Listed again in possibly October Muster of 1778. Again on 30 Dec. 1778 Muster. Listed again on Muster dated Jan. 1779 (place unknown). On March 1779 Muster at Hobuck (Hoboken), New Jersey and at Powles Hook 7 July 1779 and possibly August 1779 (location unknown) and at Governor's Island on 29 Oct. 1779 and Dec. 1779. Also on 19 March and May 1780 (location unknown). On 14 July and 11 Sept. and 2 Dec. 1780 muster at Staten Island, New York. Listed on 29 April 1781 muster at Staten Island.
Source - 4BNJVM & DSR

RAMSEY, William
Listed in 4th. Battalion New Jersey Volunteers muster roll commanded by Lt. Col. Abraham Bushkirk and Capt. Peter Ruton (Ruttan) at Staten Island, New York dated March 1778. Listed as Private. Also listed on 18 Nov. 1777 Muster at same place on command recruiting. He enlisted on 7 Dec. 1776. Again on 6 Jan. 1778 Muster at same place. Again in March and May (sick on Staten Island) and July and possibly August or September and October 1778 Muster at same place. Listed again on 30 Dec. 1778 Muster at same place as sick. And Muster dated Jan. 1779 (location unknown) and as a prisoner with Rebels. On March 1779 Muster at Hobuck (Hoboken), New Jersey and at Powles Hook 7 July 1779 and possibly August 1779 (location unknown) and at Governor's Island on 29 Oct. 1779 and Dec. 1779. Also on 19 March and May 1780 muster (location unknown) and taken prisoner on 15 Jan. 1780. On 14 July and 11 Sept. and 2 Dec. 1780 muster at Staten Island, New York (prisoner). Listed on 29 April 1781 muster at Staten Island (prisoner).

Source - 4BNJVM & DSR

RANDALL, Jonathan Capt.
Listed as Captain on his muster roll and company in His Majesty's Loyal American Regiment commanded by Col. Beverly Robinson on 27 August 1778 (location unknown).
Source - DSR2

RANZEIR, George
Listed with Sir John Johnston's Brigade and later joined Butler's Rangers. Disbanded in 1783 and possibly was granted land in Niagara, Ontario.
Source - SJJB

RATCHFORD, James
Granted with other refugee loyalist's 21,380 acres by Gov. Parr 8 Aug. 1795 (85?) in Kings County, Nova Scotia.
Source - HKC#3

RATTAN, John
Late of Sussex County, New Jersey, listed in inquisition 9 Feb. 1779 at Sussex Court of Inquiry by Isaac Martin and Samuel Meeker, Commissioners.
Source - NJNE

RATTAN, Samuel
Late of Sussex County, New Jersey, listed in inquisition 9 Feb. 1779 at Sussex Court of Inquiry by Isaac Martin and Samuel Meeker, Commissioners.
Source - NJNE

RAYMOND, Ann (Perry)
Wife of Ebenezer Raymond who was jailed in Sandwich, Massachusetts (Cape Cod) in March 1778 for being a loyalist (per Percival Diary).
Source - SA

RAYMOND, Ebenezer
He was jailed in Sandwich, Massachusetts (Cape Cod) for being a loyalist in March 1778 (per Percival Diary). He married Ann Perry.
Source - SA

RAYMOND, James Capt.
Granted with others 8,900 acres 15 Oct. 1784 by Gov. Parr in Kings County, Nova Scotia. Also listed in Gen. Skinner's muster roll, Seconded Officers (date unknown).
Source - HKC#2 & GSB

REA(?), William
Listed as Private in May 1783 Muster Roll of Lieut. Col. Stephen Delancey, commanded by Col. Cortland Skinner Esq. at New Town (location unclear).
Source - DMR

REDDING, Francis
Listed with Sir John Johnston's Brigade and later joined Joseph Brant's Volunteers. Disbanded in 1783 and possibly granted land in Niagara, Ontario.
Source - SJJB

REDNOR (Ridner), William
Listed as a Private on Muster Roll of Capt. Peter Ruttan's Company in the 4th. Battalion of New Jersey Volunteers commanded by Lieut. Col. Abraham Buskirk Esq. Possibly in Jan. 1779 (place unknown). Also on muster 19 March and May 1780 (location unknown). On 14 July and 11 Sept. and 2 Dec. 1780 muster at Staten Island, New York. Listed on 29 April 1781 muster at Staten Island.
Source - DSR

REED(?), George
Listed as Private in command on muster roll of Capt. William Gray's company of New York Volunteers from 24 Feb. to 24 April 1781, location unknown.
Source - DSR3

REED (Read), John
Listed as Private on muster roll of Capt. Christopher Hatch's Company of Loyal Americans, commanded by Col. Beverly Robinson at Haarlem, New York, possibly at beginning of 1778 and on 21 April 1778 as on prisoners Barrack Guard duty.
Source - DSR2

REED, Moses
Listed as Private at Comm. Loyds Neck on muster roll of Capt. Jonathan Randall's company in His Majesty's Loyal American Regiment commanded by Col. Beverly Robinson on 27 August 1778.
Source - DSR2

REID, John Lieut.
Granted with other loyalist refugee's 21,380 acres by Gov. Parr in Kings County, Nova Scotia 8 Aug. 1795(85?).
Source - HKC#3

REID, William Lieut
Granted with other refugee loyalists 21,380 acres by Gov. Parr 8 Aug. 1795 (85?) in Kings County, Nova Scotia.
Source - HKC#3

REYNOLDS, Benjamin
Listed with Sir John Johnston's Brigade and later joined Joseph Brant's Volunteers. Disbanded in 1783 and possibly granted land in Niagara, Ontario.
Source - SJJB

REYNOLDS, Thomas
Listed as Private on muster roll of Capt. John Howard's company of New York Volunteers commanded by Lieut. Col. George Turnbull Esq., Commandant at Paulus Hook, February 1778.
Source - DSR3

REYNOLDS, William
Listed with Sir John Johnston's Brigade and later joined Joseph Brant's Volunteers. Disbanded in 1783 and possibly granted land in Niagara, Ontario. (could this be same man as listed below?)
Source - SJJB

REYNOLDS, William
Listed as loyalist settler in Cornwall, Ontario in 1790's with 2 dependants.
Source - LCO

RICE, Jesse (Dr.)
A physician from Rindge, NH. The New Hampshire General Assembly listed him and 75 others as the enemy in Nov. 1778.
Source - NHL

RICHARDSON, Thomas
Listed in New Jersey Volunteers muster roll commanded by Col. Joseph Barton and Capt. James Shaw dated 26 Jan. 1777.
Source - NJM

RIDDLE, Colonel James
Loyalist from Surry County, North Carolina.
Source - JWC

RIDNER, Abel
Listed in 4th. Battalion New Jersey Volunteers muster roll commanded by Lt. Col. Abraham Bushkirk and Capt. Peter Ruton (Ruttan)at Staten Island, New York dated March 1778. Listed as Private who died 26 Feb. 1778. Listed again on 6 Jan. 1778 Muster at same place.
Source - 4BNJVM & DSR

RIDNER, Henry
Listed in 4th. Battalion New Jersey Volunteers muster roll commanded by Lt. Col. Abraham Bushkirk and Capt. Peter Ruton at Staten Island, New York dated March 1778. Listed as Private and discharged.
Source - 4BNJVM & DSR

RIDNER (Rithner)(Ridnor)(Rednor), Peter
Listed in 4th. Battalion New Jersey Volunteers muster roll commanded by Lt. Col. Abraham Buskirk and Capt. Peter Ruton (Ruttan) at Staten Island, New York dated March 1778. Listed as a Corporal and sick. Also listed on 18 Nov. 1777 Muster at same place. He enlisted on 7 Dec. 1776. Again on 6 Jan. 1778 Muster at same place as sick and in quarters. Again in March and May and July and possibly August or September and October 1778 Muster at same place still sick. Again on 30 Dec. 1778 Muster as being on guard. Also listed on Jan. 1779 Muster (place unknown). On March 1779 Muster at Hobuck (Hoboken), New Jersey and at Powles Hook 7 July 1779 and possibly August 1779 (location unknown) and at Governor's Island on 29 Oct. 1779 and Dec. 1779. Also on 19 March and May 1780 muster (location unknown). On 14 July and 11 Sept. and 2 Dec. 1780 muster at Staten Island, New York. Listed on 29 April 1781 muster at Staten Island.
Source - 4BNJVM & DSR

RIKERT, Paul
Listed as Private on muster roll of Capt. John Howard's company of New York Volunteers commanded by Lieut. Col. George Turnbull Esq., Commandant at Paulus Hook, February 1778.
Source - DSR3

RINES, John
Granted 100 acres in Rive Mile River, Nova Scotia under Major General Small. Also another listed for a John getting 300 acres at same place.
Source - WWRD

RINES, Thomas
Granted 300 acres at Five-Mile River, Nova Scotia under Major General Small.
Source - WWRD

RINES, Williams
Granted 300 acres in Five-Mile River, Nova Scotia under Major General Small.
Source - WWRD

RINUEL(?), James Capt.
Listed in Gen. Skinner's Brigade muster roll, Seconded Officers (date unknown) at age 46 from America. Served 7 years in Provincial Corps..
Source - GSB

RITHNER, Able
Listed as a Private on 18 Nov. 1777 Muster Roll of Capt. Peter Ruttan's Company, the 4th. Battalion of New Jersey Volunteers commanded by Col. Abraham Bushkirk at Staten Island, New York. He enlisted on 7 Dec. 1776.
Source - DSR

ROBINS, Reuben
Listed as Private on muster roll of Capt. William Gray's company of New York Volunteers from 24 Feb. to 24 April 1781, location unknown.
Source - DSR3

ROBINSON, John
Listed as Lieutenant on muster roll of Major Thomas Barclay's company in the Loyal American Regiment commanded by Col. Beverly Robinson at Guanus on 11 May 1782.

Source - DSR2

ROBINSON, Robert
A Merchant. New Hampshire General Assembly listed him and 75 others as the enemy in Nov. 1778. His home was a Portsmouth, NH. Was an ensign in the Loyal American Regiment.
Source - NHL

ROCKWELL, John
Listed as loyalist settler in Cornwall, Ontario in 1790's alone.
Source - LCO

RODNEY, George B.
Listed as Sergeant on muster roll of Major Thomas Barclay's company in the Loyal American Regiment commanded by Col. Beverly Robinson at Guanus on 11 May 1782.
Source - DSR2

ROGERS, James
Listed on act of confiscation in New Hampshire on 28 Nov. 1778.
Source - NHL

ROGERS, Robert Major
New Hampshire General Assembly listed him and 75 others as the enemy in Nov. 1778. Home was in Portsmouth, NH.
Source - NHL

ROGERS, William
Listed as Private on muster roll of Major Thomas Barclay's company in the Loyal American Regiment commanded by Col. Beverly Robinson at Guanus on 11 May 1782.
Source - DSR2

ROKMEN(?), Frederick Phillips
Listed as Ensign on muster roll of Capt. Jonathan Randall's company in His Majesty's Loyal American Regiment commanded by Col. Beverly Robinson on 27 August 1778 (location unknown).
Source - DSR2

ROMYNE (Romine), (Jacom) Jacob
Listed as a Private on Muster Roll of Capt. Peter Ruton's Company in the 4th. Battalion of New Jersey Volunteers commanded by Lieut. Col.

Abraham Buskirk (Bushkirk) at Staten Island, New York in May and July and possibly August or September and October and 30 Dec. (as sick) 1778 and again on Jan. 1779 Muster (place unknown). On March 1779 Muster at Hobuck (Hoboken), New Jersey and at Powles Hook 7 July 1779, and possibly August 1779 absent with leave to New York and at Governor's Island on 29 Oct. 1779 and Dec. 1779. Also on 19 March and May 1780 muster (location unknown). On 14 July and 11 Sept. and 2 Dec. 1780 muster at Staten Island, New York. Listed on 29 April 1781 muster at Staten Island.
Source - DSR

ROSS, Alexander
From Falmouth, Maine or Massachusetts? Was a mariner. Wife was Elizabeth Tyng, daughter of Elizabeth and William Tyng.
Source - DH

ROSS, John
Listed on muster roll of First Battalion of Maryland Loyalists 11 July 1778 at Long Island, New York. Enlisted 1 Jan. 1778. Deserted 3 July 1778.
Source - ML

ROSS, Thomas
From Falmouth, Maine or Massachusetts? Died 1804. Was a mariner. Left for Grand Manan Island, Canada. Was banished and lost property in Cumberland County, Massachusetts. Left in 1781 and discharged in 1785.
Source - DH

ROWALL, William
Listed as Private and "Absent without leave" on muster roll of Major Thomas Barclay's company in the Loyal American Regiment commanded by Col. Beverly Robinson at Guanus on 11 May 1782.
Source - DSR2

ROWLAND, John M. Chaplain
Listed in Gen. Skinner's Brigade muster roll, Seconded Officers (date unknown).
Source - GSB

ROYS, Evan
Listed as loyalist settler in Cornwall, Ontario in 1790's alone.
Source - LCO

RUINTON, Hugh
Of Londonderry, New Hampshire settled after the war in New Brunswick in 1783.
Source - NHL

RUMMERFIELD, Anthony
Listed on land grant petition with others 12 July 1793 to John Graves Simcoe, Esq. for land located between Long Point and Turkey Point on the west side of Lake Erie.
Source - EGRS

RUTON (Rutan)(Ruttan), Abraham
Listed in Muster Roll of Capt. Peter Ruton's Company in the 4th. Battalion of New Jersey Volunteers commanded by Lieut. Col. Abraham Bushkirk at Staten Island, New York in May and July (listed as a Sergeant) 1778. Listed again on possibly August or September, October 1778 at ye LightHouse. Again on 30 Dec. 1778. And on Muster dated Jan. 1779 (location unknown) as a prisoner with the Rebels. On March 1779 Muster at Hobuck (Hoboken), New Jersey and at Powles Hook 7 July 1779 and again on August 1779 muster, but as a prisoner taken on 19 Aug. 1779 and at Governor's Island on 29 Oct. 1779 still prisoner. Also on 19 March and May 1780 muster (as prisoner)(location unknown). On 14 July and 11 Sept. and 2 Dec. 1780 muster at Staten Island, New York (prisoner). Listed on 29 April 1781 muster at Staten Island (prisoner).
Source - DSR

RUTON (Ruttan), Peter Capt.
Listed in 4th. Battalion New Jersey Volunteers muster roll commanded by Lt. Col. Abraham Bushkirk and himself at Staten Island, New York dated March 1778. Also listed on 18 Nov. 1777 Muster at same place and 6 Jan. 1778. Again in March 1778 Muster at same place. Again in May 1778 and on leave in New York. And again in May and possibly August or September, October and 30 Dec. 1778 at same place and again on Jan. 1779 Muster (place unknown). On March 1779 Muster at Hobuck (Hoboken), New Jersey and at Powles Hook 7 July 1779 and possibly August 1779 (location not known) and at Governor's Island on 29 Oct. 1779 and Dec. 1779. Also on 19 March and May 1780 muster as "Under arrest" (location unknown). On 14 July and 11 Sept. and 2 Dec. 1780 muster at Staten Island, New York and says he is still under arrest in New York. Listed on 29 April 1781 muster at Staten Island, but still under arrest in New York.
Source - 4BNJVM & DSR

RYAN, John
Granted 500 acres in Rawdon/Douglas, Nova Scotia under Major General Small.
Source - WWRD

RYLEY, Barnard
Listed as a Private in the General Hospital (possibly New York) on Muster Roll of Capt. Peter Ruttan's Company in the 4th. Battalion of New Jersey Volunteers commanded by Lieut. Col. Abraham Buskirk Esq. (place unknown) Jan. 1779. Listed again on 2 Dec. 1780 muster at Staten Island, New York, sick in the hospital. On 29 April 1781 muster at Staten Island, but noted that he was "on board Sloop Neptune".
Source - DSR

RYSAM, William Johnson
A Mariner. New Hampshire General Assembly listed him and 75 others as the enemy in Nov. 1778. His home was at Portsmouth, NH. On confiscation list of 28 Nov. 1778.
Source - NHL

SANDS, Edward Quartermaster
(not known if he was from New Hampshire). He became a leading merchant of the City of Saint John, New Brunswick after 1783.
Source - NHL

SARVENIER, James
Listed as a Lieutenant in Col. Abraham Bushkirk's 4th. Battalion of New Jersey Volunteers Muster Roll in Capt. Peter Ruttan's Company dated 18 Nov. 1777 at Staten Island, New York. Again in March and May and July 1778 Muster at same place. (see Servenier also)
Source - DSR

SAUNDERS, William
Listed as Private on muster roll of Capt. John Howard's company of New York Volunteers commanded by Lieut. Col. George Turnbull Esq., Commandant at Paulus Hook, February 1778.
Source - DSR3

SAWYER, Eleazer
A yeoman from Keene, NH. The New Hampshire General Assembly listed him and 75 others as the enemy in Nov. 1778.
Source - NHL

SCANLIN, John
Listed as loyalist settler in Cornwall, Ontario in 1790's alone, but later went to Montreal, Quebec.
Source - LCO

SCHADGAL, Henry
Listed as Private at Comm. Loyds Neck on muster roll of Capt. Jonathan Randall's company in His Majesty's Loyal American Regiment commanded by Col. Beverly Robinson on 27 August 1778.
Source - DSR2

SCOTT, Alexander
Granted 500 acres in Nine-Mile River, which is ten miles west of Shubenacadie.
Source - WWRD

SCOTT, Daniel
Listed with Sir John Johnston's Brigade and later joined Joseph Brant's Volunteers. Disbanded in 1783 and possibly granted land in Niagara, Ontario.
Source - SJJB

SCRIVER, Baltus
Listed as Private on muster roll of Capt. John Howard's company of New York Volunteers commanded by Lieut. Col. George Turnbull Esq., Commandant at Paulus Hook, February 1778. And again on muster of Capt. William Gray (same company) from 24 Feb. to 24 April 1781, location unknown.
Source - DSR3

SEIFER, John
From Tryon County, New York near the Mohawk river and was a tenant to Sir John Johnson. Taken prisoner in April 1780.
Source - HP

SELLIMSER, Nicholas
Listed as loyalist settler in Cornwall, Ontario in 1790's with 4 dependants on his land.
Source - LCO

SERINE, Jacob
Listed as Private "with ye Cha?? " on muster roll of Capt. Jonathan Randall's company in His Majesty's Loyal American Regiment commanded by Col. Beverly Robinson on 27 August 1778 (location unknown).
Source - DSR2

SERVENIER (Sarvenier), James Lieut.
Listed in 4th. Battalion New Jersey Volunteers muster roll commanded by Lt. Col. Abraham Bushkirk and Capt. Peter Ruton (Ruttan) at Staten Island, New York dated March 1778. Also listed on 6 Jan. 1778 Muster at same place. (Probably the same person as above Sarvenear). Listed again on possible Muster of August or September, October and 30 Dec. 1778. He appears again on Muster dated Jan. 1779 (location unknown). On March 1779 Muster at Hobuck (Hoboken), New Jersey and at Powles Hook 7 July 1779. On possible August 1779 Muster and as a prisoner with the Rebels since 19 August 1779 and at Governor's Island on 29 Oct. 1779, prisoner with the Rebels and in Dec. 1779 muster and again on 19 March and May 1780 (location unknown). On 14 July and 11 Sept. and 2 Dec. 1780 muster (as prisoner) muster at Staten Island, New York. Listed on 29 April 1781 muster at Staten Island.
Source - 4BNJVM & DSR

SHAW, Arthur
Late of Sussex County, New Jersey, listed in inquisition 9 Feb. 1779 at Sussex Court of Inquiry by Isaac Martin and Samuel Meeker, Commissioners.
Source - NJNE

SHAW, Benjamin
Was listed as a loyalist but stayed in Sandwich, Massachusetts (Cape Cod) (mentioned by source, Betsey Keene material).
Source - SA

SHAW, Eli
Listed as Private on muster roll of Capt. Christopher Hatch's Company of Loyal Americans, commanded by Col. Beverly Robinson at Haarlem, New York, possibly at beginning of 1778 and again on 21 April 1778.
Source - DSR2

SHAW, James Capt.
Listed as Captain in New Jersey Volunteers muster roll commanded by Col. Joseph Barton and is listed 5 times with dates ranging from 20 March, 1 and 4 April 1777. (could be person listed below?)
Source - NJM

SHAW, James
Late of Sussex County, New Jersey, listed in inquisition 9 Feb. 1779 at Court of Inquiry at Sussex by Isaac Martin and Samuel Meeker, Commissioners.
Source - NJNE

SHEEK, Christian
Listed as loyalist settler in Cornwall, Ontario in 1790's.
Source - LCO

SHEFER, John
Listed in Turloch, Tryon County, New York Militia 1775-77 and later in the Kings Royal Rangers of New York.
Source - SJJB

SHELL, John
Listed in Turloch, Tryon County, New York Militia 1775-77 and later in the Kings Royal Rangers of New York.
Source - SJJB

SHELLY, Abraham
Listed on muster roll of First Battalion of Maryland Loyalist 11 July 1778 in Long Island, New York. Enlisted on 6 Nov. 1777.
Source - ML

SHERWOOD, William
Listed as Private with Col. Innes on muster roll of Capt. Jonathan Randall's company in His Majesty's Loyal American Regiment commanded by Col. Beverly Robinson on 27 August 1778.
Source - DSR2

SHIELDS, James
Listed as Private in May 1783 Muster Roll of Lieut. Col. Stephen Delancey, commanded by Col. Cortland Skinner Esq. at New Town (location unclear).
Source - DMR

SHIELDS, John
Granted 500 acres in Rawdon/Douglas, Nova Scotia under Major General Small.
Sources - WWRD

SHIPPY, Zebulon
Listed on land grant petition with others 12 July 1793 to John Graves Simcoe, Esq. for land located between Long Point and Turkey Point on the west side of Lake Erie.
Source - EGRS

SHUGT, John
Listed as a Private who recruited on 29 Jan. 1779 and was on Muster Roll of Capt. Peter Ruton's Company in the 4th. Battalion of New Jersey Volunteers commanded by Lieut Col. Abraham Buskirk at Hobuck (Hoboken), New Jersey March 1779.

SHULTIS (Shults), Henry
Listed in 4th. Battalion New Jersey Volunteers muster roll commanded by Lt. Col. Abraham Bushkirk and Capt. Peter Ruton (Ruttan) at Staten Island, New York dated March 1778. Listed as Private. Also listed on 18 Nov. 1777 Muster at same place. He enlisted 22 Jan. 1777. Listed again on 6 Jan. 1778 Muster at same place. Again in March and May and July and possibly August or September (noted that he was dead 22 June) 1778.
Source - 4BNJVM & DSR

SHUMACKER (Shumaker)(Shomocker)(Shoemaker), Balthes (Baltas)(Baltis)
Listed in 4th. Battalion New Jersey Volunteers muster roll commanded by Lt. Col. Abraham Bushkirk and Capt. Peter Ruton (Ruttan) at Staten Island, New York dated March 1778. Listed as Private and sick at New York. Also listed on 18 Nov. 1777 Muster at same place as being sick and in the General Hospital. He enlisted on 7 Dec. 1776. Listed again on 6 Jan. 1778 Muster as still sick in same hospital. Again in March and May 1778, still sick in New York and in July and possibly August or September (on Furlow).
Source - 4BNJVM & DSR

SICKELS (Sickells), John
Listed as a Private on Muster Roll of Capt. Peter Ruton's Company in the 4th. Battalion of New Jersey Volunteers commanded by Lieut. Col. Abraham Buskirk (Bushkirk) at Staten Island, New York in May and July

and possibly August or September and October and 30 Dec. 1778. It says he was a Taylor at Harlem. Listed again on Muster dated Jan. 1779 (location unknown). On March 1779 Muster at Hobuck (Hoboken), New Jersey and at Powles Hook 7 July 1779 and again on August 1779 muster in same company and at Governor's Island on 29 Oct. and Dec. (Furlow)1779. Also on 19 March and May 1780 muster (location unknown). On 14 July and 11 Sept. and 2 Dec. 1780 muster at Staten Island, New York. Listed on 29 April 1781 muster at Staten Island.
Source - DSR

SIGHTS, Joseph
Listed as a Drummer who recruited on 29 Aug. 1778 and is on Muster Roll of Capt. Peter Ruton's Company in the 4th. Battalion of New Jersey Volunteers commanded by Lieut. Col. Abraham Buskirk at Staten Island, New York possibly in October 1778. Also on 30 Dec. 1778 Muster at same place. Listed again in Jan. 1779 Muster (location unknown). On March 1779 Muster at Hobuck (Hoboken), New Jersey and at Powles Hook 7 July 1779. On possible August 1779 Muster (location unknown) and at Governor's Island on 29 Oct. 1779 and Dec. 1779. Also on muster 19 March and May 1780 (location unknown). On 14 July and 11 Sept. and 2 Dec. 1780 muster at Staten Island, New York. Listed on 29 April 1781 muster at Staten Island.
Source - DSR

SIMON, Michael
Listed in New Jersey Volunteers muster roll commanded by Col. Joseph Barton and Capt. James Shaw dated 30 Jan. 1777.
Source - NJM

SIMPSON, Eliphitet
Listed as Private on muster roll of Capt. William Gray's company of New York Volunteers from 24 Feb. to 24 April 1781, location unknown.
Source - DSR3

SIMSANY (?), Robert Major
Listed on Gen. Skinner's Brigade muster roll of Seconded Officers (date unknown).
Source - GSB

SINCLAIR, William Surgeon
Listed in First Battalion of Maryland Loyalists muster roll 11 July 1778 at Long Island, New York.
Source - ML

SINGER, John
Granted 500 acres in Rawdon/Douglas, Nova Scotia under Major General Small. Another John listed as getting 500 acres in Rawdon/Douglas, Nova Scotia under Major General Small.
Source - WWRD

SINGER, Margaret
Listed with no amount of grant in Rawdon/Douglas, Nova Scotia under Major General Small.
Source - WWRD

SINGER, William
Listed in grants, but no info. noted in Rawdon/Douglas, Nova Scotia under Major General Small.
Source - WWRD

SISSILE, James
Listed as Private on muster roll of Capt. John Howard's company of New York Volunteers commanded by Lieut. Col. George Turnbull Esq., Commandant at Paulus Hook, February 1778.
Source - DSR3

SITES (Sithe) (Sithes) (Sythe), Nicholass (Nicholas)
Listed as a Private on 18 Nov. 1777 Muster Roll of the 4th. Battalion of New Jersey Volunteers commanded by Col. Abraham Bushkirk in Company of Capt. Peter Ruttan (Ruttan) at Staten Island, New York. He enlisted on 7 Dec. 1776 and was on command as a Taylor. Again listed on 6 Jan. and May and July 1778 Muster at same place. Listed again on possibly August or September Muster of 1778 as dead.
Source - DSR

SLINGERLAND, Derrick
Listed with Sir John Johnston's Brigade and later joined Butler's Rangers. Disbanded in 1783 and possibly got land grant in Niagara, Ontario.
Source - SJJB

SLINGERLAND, Tunis
Listed with Sir John Johnston's Brigade and later joined Butler's Rangers. Disbanded in 1783 and possibly was granted land in Niagara, Ontario.
Source - SJJB

SLYTHE (Slithye), Peter
Listed in 4th. Battalion New Jersey Volunteers muster roll commanded by Lt. Col. Abraham Bushkirk and Capt. Peter Ruton (Ruttan) at Staten Island, New York dated March 1778. Listed as Private and a prisoner by the rebels. Also listed on 18 Nov. 1777 Muster at same place and as taken prisoner on 22 Aug. 1777. He enlisted on 7 Dec. 1776. Again on 6 Jan. 1778 Muster at same place and still prisoner.
Source - 4BNJVM & DSR

SMITH, Francis
Listed as a Private on Muster Roll of Capt. Peter Ruton's Company in the 4th. Battalion of New Jersey Volunteers commanded by Lieut. Col. Abraham Buskirk (Bushkirk) at Staten Island, New York in July and possibly August or September (with Artillery)1778. Again in October 1778 Muster at same place as an additional Gunner. Again on 30 Dec. 1778 Muster. On March 1779 Muster at Hobuck (Hoboken), New Jersey and at Powles Hook 7 July 1779. On possible August 1779 Muster (place unknown) and at Governor's Island on 29 Oct. 1779 and Dec. 1779, listed as deserted.
Source - DSR

SMITH, George
Listed in 4th. Battalion New Jersey Volunteers muster roll commanded by Lt. Col. Abraham Bushkirk and Capt. Peter Ruton (Ruttan) at Staten Island, New York dated March 1778. Listed as Private. Also listed on 18 Nov. 1777 Muster at same place as a Private. He enlisted on 29 May 1777. Again listed on 6 Jan. 1778 Muster at same place. Again in March, May, July and possibly August or September, October and 30 Dec. 1778 Muster at same place. Also in Jan. 1779 Muster (place unknown) Muster, but on board the ship, Sloop Nipten. On March 1779 Muster at Hobuck (Hoboken), New Jersey and at Powles Hook 7 July 1779. On possible August 1779 Muster (place unknown) and at Governor's Island on 29 Oct. 1779 and Dec. 1779. Also on 19 March and May 1780 muster (location unknown). On 14 July and 11 Sept. and 2 Dec. 1780 muster at Staten Island, New York. Listed on 29 April 1781 muster at Staten Island.
Source - 4BNJVM & DSR

SMITH, Hans
Listed in New Jersey Volunteers muster roll commanded by Col. Joseph Barton and Capt. James Shaw dated 4 April 1777.
Source - NJM

SMITH, John
A Mariner. New Hampshire General Assembly listed him and 75 others as the enemy in Nov. 1778. His home was at Portsmouth, NH.
Source - NHL

SMITH, John
Granted with other refugee loyalist's 21, 380 acres by Gov. Parr 8 Aug. 1795 (85?) in Kings County, Nova Scotia.
Source - HKC#3

SMITH, Peter
Listed in 4th. Battalion New Jersey Volunteers muster roll commanded by Lt. Col. Abraham Bushkirk and Capt. Peter Ruton (Ruttan) at Staten Island, New York dated March 1778. Listed as Private and on guard duty. Also listed on 18 Nov. 1777 Muster at same place. He enlisted on 29 May 1777. Again listed on 6 Jan. 1778 Muster at same place. Again in March and May and July 1778 and on guard and possibly August or September, October and 30 Dec. 1778. Also on Jan. 1779 (location unknown) Muster Roll and as being on the ship, Sloop Nipten. On March 1779 Muster at Hobuck (Hoboken), New Jersey and at Powles Hook 7 July 1779 and again on August 1779 muster in same company, but taken prisoner on 19 Aug. 1779 and at Governor's Island on 29 Oct. and Dec. 1779 still prisoner. Listed again on 19 March and May 1780 muster as "joined the Battalion again" (location unknown). On 14 July and 11 Sept. and 2 Dec. 1780 muster at Staten Island, New York. Listed on 29 April 1781 muster at Staten Island.
Source - 4BNJVM & DSR

SMITH, Thomas
Listed as a Private who enlisted 2 Nov. 1778 on Muster Roll of Capt. Peter Rutton's Company in the 4th. Battalion of New Jersey Volunteers commanded by Lieut. Col. Abraham Buskirk at Staten Island, New York on 30 Dec. 1778. On March 1779 Muster at Hobuck (Hoboken), New Jersey and at Powles Hook 7 July 1779 and again on August 1779 muster listed as a deserter on 14 July 1779.
Source - DSR

SMITH, Thomas
A yeoman from Londonderry, NH. The New Hampshire General Assembly listed him and 75 others as the enemy in Nov. 1778.
Source - NHL

SMITH, William
Listed as a Private on Muster Roll of Capt. Peter Ruton's Company in the 4th. Battalion of New Jersey Volunteers commanded by Lieut. Col. Abraham Buskirk (Bushkirk) at Staten Island, New York in May and July 1778. Says he was on Furlow and deserted. Again listed on possibly August or September Muster 1778 and on Furlow. Listed again in October and 30 Dec. 1778 at same place as recruiting country and on Jan. 1779 Muster (location unknown) still recruiting. On March 1779 Muster at Hobuck (Hoboken), New Jersey and at Powles Hook 7 July 1779 and on August 1779 muster in same company and at Governor's Island on 29 Oct. 1779 listed as in the country and Dec. 1779 as deserted. Also on 19 March and May 1780 muster (location unknown) on command recruiting. On 14 July and 11 Sept. and 2 Dec. 1780 muster at Staten Island, New York. Listed on 29 April 1781 muster at Staten Island (recruiting).
Source - DSR

SNIDER, John
Listed on muster roll of First Battalion of Maryland Loyalists 11 July 1778 at Long Island, New York. Enlisted 30 Nov. 1777.
Source - ML

SNOW, Benjamin
Graduate of Dartmouth College in New Hampshire arrived at Annapolis Royal, Nova Scotia on the ship, Amphitrite in Oct. 1783. The following year he opened a grammar school near there.
Source - NHL

SOMMER, John Peter, Lieutenant
From Turloch, Tyron Co., New York. Served in Turloch Militia under Capt. Jacob Miller 1775-77, then later transferred to First Battalion, Kings Royal Rangers, New York. Possibly settled around Williamsburgh, Ontario.
Source - SJJB

SOMMER, Wilhelm
Listed in Turloch, Tryon County, New York Militia 1775-77 and later in the Kings Royal Rangers of New York.

Source - SJJB

SOULE, Howland
Listed as Private who died 4 Aug. 1777 on muster roll of Capt. William Gray's company of New York Volunteers from 24 Feb. to 24 April 1781, location unknown.
Source - DSR3

SPARHAWK, Andrew Pepperell Esq.
New Hampshire General Assembly listed him and 75 others as the enemy in Nov. 1778. His home was at Portsmouth, NH.
Source - NHL

SPICER, Robert Lieut.
Granted with other refugee loyalist's 21, 380 acres by Gov. Parr 8 Aug. 1795 (85?) in Kings County, Nova Scotia.
Source - HKC#3

SPRINGER, Henry
Listed as Private on muster roll of Capt. Christopher Hatch's Company of Loyal Americans, commanded by Col. Beverly Robinson at Haarlem, New York, possibly at beginning of 1778 and on 21 April 1778.
Source - DSR2

STACKHOUSE, Aalia(?)
Listed as Private on muster roll of Capt. John Howard's company of New York Volunteers commanded by Lieut. Col. George Turnbull Esq., Commandant at Paulus Hook, February 1778.
Source - DSR3

STAGLER, William
Listed as Corporal on muster roll of Capt. John Howard's company of New York Volunteers commanded by Lieut. Col. George Turnbull Esq., Commandant at Paulus Hook, February 1778.
Source - DSR3

STAKER, Natheist (Nautes)(Nautis)(Ignatius)
Listed in 4th. Battalion New Jersey Volunteers muster roll commanded by Lt. Col. Abraham Bushkirk and Capt. Peter Ruton (Ruttan) at Staten Island, New York dated March 1778. Listed as Private and sick in New York. Also listed on 18 Nov. 1777 Muster at same place saying he enlisted on 7 Dec. 1776. Again listed on 6 Jan. 1778 Muster at same place

as sick in General Hospital. Again in March and May 1778, still sick in NY and July and possibly August or September and October 1778. Listed again at same place 30 Dec. 1778 and sick and possibly discharged. He does show up on Jan. 1779 Muster Roll as being at Regiment Hospital. On March 1779 Muster at Hobuck (Hoboken), New Jersey and at Powles Hook 7 July 1779 and again on August 1779 muster in same company and at Governor's Island on 29 Oct. 1779. Also on 19 March and May 1780 muster (location unknown). On 14 July and 11 Sept. and 2 Dec. 1780 muster at Staten Island, New York. Listed on 29 April 1781 muster at Staten Island.
Source - 4BNJVM & DSR

STARBUCK, Samuel
From Nantucket, Massachusetts (Cape Cod & Islands). Was a whale fisherman. Had trial for treason in 1779. Left in 1783 for Nova Scotia. (also see Timothy Folger for more info.)
Source - DH & LMTMPC

STARK, John
A yeoman from Dunbarton, NH. The New Hampshire General Assembly list him and 75 others as the enemy in Nov. 1778. Listed with William Stark Esq... Was a Lieut. in the Royal Guides and Pioneers.
Source - NHL

STARK, William Esq.
Received a colonel's commission in the royal army after refusing to join one of the New Hampshire Patriot regiments. From Dunbarton, NH. The New Hampshire General Assembly listed him with 75 others as the enemy in Nov. 1778. John Stark listed with him.
Source - NHL

STAVERS, Bartholomew
A Post-rider. New Hampshire General Assembly listed him and 75 others as the enemy in Nov. 1778. His home was at Portsmouth, NH.
Source - NHL

STEENBURUGH(?), Peter
Listed as Private on muster roll of Capt. John Howard's company of New York Volunteers commanded by Lieut. Col. George Turnbull Esq., Commandant at Paulus Hook, February 1778.
Source - DSR3

STEENBURUGH(?), William
Listed as Private on muster roll of Capt. John Howard's company of New York Volunteers commanded by Lieut. Col. George Turnbull Esq., Commandant at Paulus Hook, February 1778.
Source - DSR3

STEINBARRACK, John
Listed as Drummer on muster roll of Capt. William Gray's company of New York Volunteers from 24 Feb. to 24 April 1781, location unknown.
Source - DSR3

STEINBERG, Cornellius
Listed as Private on muster roll of Major Thomas Barclay's company in the Loyal American Regiment commanded by Col. Beverly Robinson at Guanus on 11 May 1782.
Source - DSR2

STEINBURGH, Abraham
Listed as Drummer on muster roll of Capt. John Howard's company of New York Volunteers commanded by Lieut. Col. George Turnbull Esq., Commandant at Paulus Hook, February 1778. Listed again on muster of Capt. William Gray (same company) from 24 Feb. to 24 April 1781, location unknown.
Source - DSR3

STEINBURGH, Simeon
Listed as Private on muster roll of Capt. Christopher Hatch's Company of Loyal Americans, commanded by Col. Beverly Robinson at Haarlem, New York, possibly at beginning of 1778 and again on 21 April 1778.
Source - DSR2

STEINBURGH, William
Listed as Private on muster roll of Capt. William Gray's company of New York Volunteers from 24 Feb. to 24 April 1781, location unknown.
Source - DSR3

STERLING, William Ensign
Listed on muster roll of First Battalion of Maryland Loyalists, 11 July 1778 at Long Island, New York.
Source - ML

STEVENS, Enos
A gentleman from Charlestown, NH (listed with Solomon and Phineas Stevens). The New Hampshire General Assembly listed him and 75 others as the enemy in Nov. 1778. On confiscation list of 28 Nov. 1778. On petition with Phineas to change Conway to Digby, Nova Scotia in honor of Rear Admiral Robert Digby on 20 Feb. 1784. Later, he settled at Weymouth which was 17 miles south of Digby.
Source - NHL

STEVENS, Isaiah
Listed as Sergeant on muster roll of Capt. Christopher Hatch's Company of Loyal Americans, commanded by Col. Beverly Robinson at Haarlem, New York, possibly at beginning of 1778 and again on 21 April 1778.
Source - DSR2

STEVENS, Phineas (Dr.)
A physician from Charlestown, NH.(listed with Enos and Solomon Stevens). The New Hampshire General Assembly listed him and 75 others as the enemy in Nov. 1778. On petition with Enos to change Conway to Digby, Nova Scotia after Rear Admiral Robert Digby 20 Feb. 1784. Later, he settled at Weymouth which was 17 miles south of Digby.
Source - NHL

STEVENS (Stephens), Solomon
A yeoman from Charlestown, NH. The New Hampshire General Assembly listed him and 75 others as the enemy in Nov. 1778. He settled at Musquash, New Brunswick and died there in 1819.
Source - NHL

STEWART, James
Listed as Corporal on muster roll of Capt. Christopher Hatch's Company of Loyal Americans, commanded by Col. Beverly Robinson at Haarlem, New York, possibly at beginning of 1778 and again on 21 April 1778.(could this person be the same as listed below James Stewart?)
Source - DSR2

STEWART, James Capt.
Granted with other refugee loyalist's 21, 380 acres by Gov. Parr 8 Aug. 1795 (85?) in Kings County, Nova Scotia.
Source - HKC#3

STINE, John
Listed in New Jersey Volunteers muster roll commanded by Col. Joseph Barton and Capt. James Shaw dated 6 March 1777.
Source - NJM

STINSON, John Jr.
From Dunbarton, NH. The New Hampshire General assembly list him and 75 others as the enemy in Nov. 1778. Samuel Stinson listed with him. On confiscation list of 28 Nov. 1778. One record says he was from Hillsboro, NH. He served a short time in the Royal American Reformers. He went to Saint John, Nova Scotia (New Brunswick) in May 1783 and spent a year at Maugerville, New Brunswick and was granted land and settled at Lincoln, Sunbury County, New Brunswick.
Source - NHL

STINSON, Samuel
From Dunbarton, NH. The New Hampshire General Assembly list him and 75 others as the enemy in Nov. 1778. John Stinson Jr. listed with him.
Source - NHL

STIRR (Sturr), Michael
Listed in 4th. Battalion New Jersey Volunteers muster roll commanded by Lt. Col. Abraham Bushkirk and Capt. Peter Ruton (Ruttan) at Staten Island, New York dated March 1778. Listed as Private and dead. Also listed on 18 Nov. 1777 Muster at same place as deceased on 1 May 1777. He enlisted on 22 Jan. 1777.
Source - 4BNJVM & DSR

STIRR (Sturr)(Stor), William
Listed in 4th. Battalion New Jersey Volunteers muster roll commanded by Lt. Col. Abraham Bushkirk and Capt. Peter Ruton (Ruttan) at Staten Island, New York dated March 1778. Listed as Private and a prisoner with the rebels. Also listed on 18 Nov. 1777 Muster at same place and as taken prisoner on 29 Dec. 1776. He enlisted on 7 Dec. 1776. Again on 6 Jan. 1778 Muster at same place and still prisoner. Listed again on October 1778 Muster at same place and enlisted 6 Dec. 1776, taken prisoner 20 Dec. 1776, returned 2 Oct. 1778 with a note; Not subsisted nor received bounty. Again on 30 Dec. 1778 Muster and Jan. 1779 (location unknown) as a prisoner with the Rebels. On March 1779 Muster at Hobuck (Hoboken), New Jersey and at Powles Hook 7 July 1779 and again on August 1779 muster, but noted that he was taken prisoner on 19 Aug.

1779 and at Governor's Island on 29 Oct. 1779 still prisoner and on Dec. 1779 muster as "has not drawn his bounty". Also on 19 March and May 1780 muster (location unknown)(prisoner). On 14 July and 11 Sept. and 2 Dec. 1780 muster at Staten Island, New York (prisoner). Listed on 29 April 1781 muster at Staten Island (prisoner).
Source - 4BNJVM & DSR

STOCKTON, Richard G. Major
Listed in Gen. Skinner's Brigade muster roll in Seconded Officers (date unknown).
Source - GSB

STONE, John
Listed on muster roll of First Battalion of Maryland Loyalists 11 July 1778 at Long Island, New York. Enlisted 6 Nov. 1777. Deserted 24 June 1778.
Source - ML

STORY, James
Listed as Private on muster roll of Capt. John Howard's company of New York Volunteers commanded by Lieut. Col. George Turnbull Esq., Commandant at Paulus Hook, February 1778. And listed on muster of Capt. William Gray (same company) from 24 Feb. to 24 April 1781, location unknown.
Source - DSR3

STOURER, James
Listed as a Private on Muster Roll of Capt. Peter Ruttan's Company commanded by Col. Abraham Bushkirk at Staten Island, New York on 18 Nov. 1777. He enlisted on 22 Jan. 1777.
Source - DSR

STOVER, Martin
Listed as Private and confined with Rebels on muster roll of Major Thomas Barclay's company in the Loyal American Regiment commanded by Col. Beverly Robinson at Guanus on 11 May 1782.
Source - DSR2

STRAIT, Thomas
Listed as Private who died on 16 April 1777 on muster roll of Capt. John Howard's company of New York Volunteers commanded by Lieut. Col. George Turnbull Esq., Commandant at Paulus Hook, February 1778.
Source - DSR3

STRANG, Gabriel
Listed as Private at Comm. Loyds Neck on muster roll of Capt. Jonathan Randall's company in His Majesty's Loyal American Regiment commanded by Col. Beverly Robinson on 27 August 1778.
Source - DSR2

STREET, Lockwood
From Tryon County, New York near the Mohawk river and was a tenant to Sir John Johnson. Taken prisoner in April 1780.
Source - HP

STUMP, John
Member of land board of Digby, Nova Scotia 1783-84.
Source - NHL

STURGE, Steven
Listed as Private, sick in quarters on muster roll of Capt. Jonathan Randall's company in His Majesty's Loyal American Regiment commanded by Col. Beverly Robinson on 27 August 1778 (location unknown).
Source - DSR2

STURSE (Sturee), James
Listed on Muster Roll of Capt. Peter Ruttan's Company in the 4th. Battalion of New Jersey Volunteers commanded by Col. Abraham Bushkirk at Staten Island, New York on 6 Jan. 1778. He was listed as a Private. (Is he the same as James Stourer above?). Also listed in July 1778 Muster at same place with note that he was dead 17 Jan. 1778 (different date from last muster roll).
Source - DSR

STUWIS, James
Listed in 4th. Battalion New Jersey Volunteers muster roll commanded by Lt. Col. Abraham Bushkirk and Capt. Peter Ruton (Ruttan)at Staten Island, New York dated March 1778. Listed as Private. Also in March 1778 Muster at same place.
Source - 4BNJVM & DSR

SUTHARD, Joseph
Listed as Private, in General Hospital on muster roll of Capt. William Gray's company of New York Volunteers from 24 Feb. to 24 April 1781, location unknown.

Source - DSR3

SWARTZ, Simon
Listed in Turloch, Tryon County, New York Militia 1775-77 and later in the Kings Royal Rangers of New York.
Source - SJJB

SWEIDS, Richard
Listed as Ensign on muster roll of Capt. Christopher Hatch's Company of Loyal Americans, commanded by Col. Beverly Robinson at possibly Haarlem, New York on 21 April 1778.
Source - DSR2

SWINDLE, Alexaner
Listed on muster roll of First Battalion of Maryland Loyalist 11 July 1778 at Long Island, New York. Enlisted on 6 Nov. 1777.
Source - ML

SYMMONS (Simmons), Calyb
Listed as Private and prisoner with the Rebels on muster roll of Capt. John Howard's company of New York Volunteers commanded by Lieut. Col. George Turbull Esq., Commandant at Paulus Hook, February 1778. Again on muster of Capt. William Gray (same company) from 24 Feb. to 24 April 1781, location unknown.
Source - DSR3

SYMMONS (Simmons), James
Listed as Private on muster roll of Capt. John Howard's company of New York Volunteers commanded by Lieut. Col. George Turnbull Esq., Commandant at Paulus Hook, February 1778. Again on muster of Capt. William Gray (same company) from 24 Feb. to 24 April 1781, location unknown.
Source - DSR3

SYMSON, Eliphlet
Listed as Private on muster roll of Capt. John Howard's company of New York Volunteers commanded by Lieut. Col. George Turnbull Esq., Commandant at Paulus Hook, February 1778.
Source - DSR3

SYTHES, Nicholas
Listed in 4th. Battalion New Jersey Volunteers muster roll commanded by Lt. Col. Abraham Bushkirk and Capt. Peter Ruton (Ruttan) at Staten Island, New York dated March 1778. Listed as Private. Also in March 1778 Muster at same place.
Source - 4BNJVM

TALLON, Joseph
Listed on muster roll of First Battalion of Maryland Loyalists 11 July 1778 at Long Island, New York. Enlisted 6 Nov. 1777.
Source - ML

TATE, Samuel
From Falmouth, Maine or Massachusetts? Was a mariner and served in Navy of Great Britain. Left the area.
Source - DH

TATE, William
From Falmouth, Maine or Massachusetts? Was a merchant. Mobbed and left for Bristol, Great Britain.
Source - DH

TARBELL, Samuel
Listed on act of confiscation in New Hampshire on 28 Nov. 1778.
Source - NHL

TAYLOR, Eleazer Lieut.
Granted with others 8,900 acres 15 Oct. 1784 by Gov. Parr in Kings County, Nova Scotia.
Source - HKC#2

TAYLOR, William Esq.
Granted with other refugee loyalist's 21, 380 acres by Gov. Parr 8 Aug. 1795 (85?) in Kings County, Nova Scotia. Excheated 14 May 1814.
Source - HKC#3

TEATHOUK, Gideon
Listed as Private with Col. Innes on muster roll of Capt. Jonathan Randall's company in His Majesty's Loyal American Regiment commanded by Col. Beverly Robinson on 27 August 1778 (location unknown).
Source - DSR2

TERBOUSCH (Terbush), Fryer (Fryor)
Listed as Private on muster roll of Capt. John Howard's company of New York Volunteers commanded by Lieut. Col. George Turnbull Esq., Commandant at Paulus Hook, February 1778. Again on muster of Capt. William Gray (same company) from 24 Feb. to 24 April 1781, location unknown.
Source - DSR3

TERWILLIGER, Ahasuerus
Listed as Private on muster roll of Major Thomas Barclay's company in the Loyal American Regiment commanded by Col. Beverly Robinson at Guanus on 11 May 1782.
Source - DSR2

THOMAS, George
Listed as Private in General Hospital on muster roll of Capt. William Gray's company of New York Volunteers from 24 Feb. to 24 April 1781, location unknown.
Source - DSR3

THOMPSON, Benjamin Esq.
Of Concord, New Hampshire later became a secretary in the Colonial Secretary's office in London. Showing his support by entertaining two British officers he was forced to leave Woburn, Massachusetts and fled to Rhode Island and later sailed to Boston in October 1775. That following January he sailed for England. New Hampshire General Assembly listed him with 75 others as the enemy in Nov. 1778. His home was at Concord, NH.
Source - NHL

THOMPSON, William
Granted with other refugee loyalist's 21, 380 acres by Gov. Parr 8 Aug. 1795 (85?) in Kings County, Nova Scotia.
Source - HKC#3

THOMSON, Georg
Listed in Turloch, Tryon County, New York Militia 1775-77 and later in the Kings Royal Rangers of New York.
Source - SJJB

THORN, Stephen
Listed as Private, on duty on muster roll of Capt. John Howard's company of New York Volunteers commanded by Lieut. Col. George Turnbull Esq., Commandant at Paulus Hook, February 1778. Also on muster of Capt. William Gray (same company) from 24 Feb. to 24 April 1781, location unknown.
Source - DSR3

TOMPKINS, Edmund
Listed as Private on muster roll of Capt. Christopher Hatch's Company of Loyal Americans, commanded by Col. Beverly Robinson at Haarlem, New York, possibly at beginning of 1778 and again on 21 April 1778, listed as dead 12 April 1778.
Source - DSR2

TOMPKINS, Elijah
Listed as Private, sick in quarters on muster roll of Capt. Jonathan Randall's company in His Majesty's Loyal American Regiment commanded by Col. Beverly Robinson on 27 August 1778 (location unknown).
Source - DSR2

TOMPKINS, Edward
Listed as Private on muster roll of Capt. Jonathan Randall's company in His Majesty's Loyal American Regiment commanded by Col. Beverly Robinson on 27 August 1778 (location unknown).
Source - DSR2

TOMPKINS, John
Listed as Corporal on muster roll of Capt. Jonathan Randall's company in His Majesty's Loyal American Regiment commanded by Col. Beverly Robinson on 27 August 1778 (location unknown).
Source - DSR2

TOMPKINS, William
Listed as Private on muster roll of Capt. Jonathan Randall's company in His Majesty's Loyal American Regiment commanded by Col. Beverly Robinson on 27 August 1778 (location unknown).
Source - DSR2

TOWNSEND, Joseph
Listed as Private on muster roll of Capt. Christopher Hatch's Company of Loyal Americans, commanded by Col. Beverly Robinson at Haarlem, New York, possibly at beginning of 1778 and on 21 April 1778, on Barrack Guard duty.
Source - DSR2

TOWNSHEND (Townsend), Henry
Listed as Private on duty on muster roll of Capt. John Howard's company of New York Volunteers commanded by Lieut. Col. George Turnbull Esq., Commandant at Paulus Hook, February 1778. Again on muster of Capt. William Gray (same company) from 24 Feb. to 24 April 1781, location unknown.
Source - DSR3

TOWSWICK, Casper
Listed with Sir John Johnston's Brigade and later joined Butler's Rangers. Disbanded in 1783 and possibly was granted land in Niagara, Ontario.
Source - SJJB

TRAILL, Robert Esq.
Was comptroller of the customs at Portsmouth, New Hampshire and was mentioned in Gov. John Wentworth's letters to his sister as being with him in Flatbush, Long Island, New York around 1777 while in exile. New Hampshire General Assembly listed him and 75 others as the enemy in Nov. 1778.
Source - NHL

TRAVIS, Jeremiah
Listed as a Drummer on muster roll of Major Thomas Barclay's company in the Loyal American Regiment commanded by Col. Beverly Robinson at Guanus on 11 May 1782.
Source - DSR2

TRAVIS, John
Listed as Corporal on muster roll of Capt. Jonathan Randall's company in His Majesty's Loyal American Regiment commanded by Col. Beverly Robinson on 27 August 1778 (location unknown).
Source - DSR2

TRAVIS (Frairs?), Nehemiah
Listed as Private on muster roll of Capt. Jonathan Randall's company in His Majesty's Loyal American Regiment commanded by Col. Beverly Robinson on 27 August 1778 (location unknown).
Source - DSR2

TRAVIS (Frairs?), Robert
Listed as Private on muster roll of Capt. Jonathan Randall's company in His Majesty's Loyal American Regiment commanded by Col. Beverly Robinson on 27 August 1778 (location unknown).
Source - DSR2

TRIVER (Traver), Bastion
Listed as Private on muster roll of Capt. John Howard's company of New York Volunteers commanded by Lieut. Col. George Turnbull Esq., Commandant at Paulus Hook, February 1778. Again on muster of Capt. William Gray (same company) from 24 Feb. to 24 April 1781, location unknown.
Source - DSR3

TRIVER (Traver), Daniel
Listed as Private on muster roll of Capt. John Howard's company commanded by Lieut. Col. George Turnbull Esq., Commandant at Paulus Hook, February 1778. Alson on muster of Capt. William Gray (same company) from 24 Feb. to 24 April 1781, location unknown.
Source - DSR3

TRIVER (Traver), George
Listed as Private on muster roll of Capt. John Howard's company of New York Volunteers commanded by Lieut. Col. George Turnbull Esq., Commandant at Paulus Hook, February 1778. Again on muster of Capt. William Gray (same company) from 24 Feb. to 24 April 1781, location unknown.
Source - DSR3

TRIVER (Traver), Jacob
Listed as Private on muster roll of Capt. John Howard's company of New York Volunteers commanded by Lieut. Col. George Turnbull Esq., Commandant at Paulus Hook, February 1778. Also on muster of Capt. William Gray (same company) from 24 Feb. to 24 April 1781, location unknown.
Source - DSR3

TRYING, Frances
He was from Sandwich, Barnstable County, Massachusetts (Cape Cod) and was part of a Tory underground and met at Seth Perry's house (see his listing) for a loyalist meeting with many others and was banished.
Source - SA

TUD(?), David
Listed as Sergeant on muster roll of Capt. William Gray's company of New York Volunteers from 24 Feb. to 24 April 1781, location unknown.
Source - DSR3

TUPPER, Benjamin
From Nantucket, Massachusetts (Cape Cod & Islands). Was a physician. Had trial for treason in 1779.
Source - DH

TUPPER, Eldad
Was listed as a loyalist in Sandwich, Massachusetts (Cape Cod), but stayed.
Source - SA

TUPPER, Isaac
Was listed as a loyalist in Sandwich, Massachusetts (Cape Cod), but stayed.
Source - SA

TUPPER, Prince
From Sandwich, Barnstable County, Massachusetts (Cape Cod). Cited by town or committee of correspondence for being a Tory in 1778. Jailed 1778-9. He was jailed for a short time at the Barnstable goal and is said to have stayed after the war.
Source - DH & SA

TUREE, James
Listed as a Private in Muster Roll of Capt. Peter Ruton's Company in the 4th. Battalion of New Jersey Volunteers commanded by Lieut. Col. Abraham Buskirk (Bushkirk) at Staten Island, New York in May 1778. Says deceased 24 April 1778,
Source - DSR

TURNER, Barnibas
Listed on muster roll of First Battalion of Maryland Loyalists 11 July 1778 at Long Island, New York. Enlisted on 24 Dec. 1777.
Source - ML

TURNER, Nathan
Listed as Private on muster roll of Capt. Jonathan Randall's company in His Majesty's Loyal American Regiment commanded by Col. Beverly Robinson on 27 August 1778 (location unknown).
Source - DSR2

TUTTLE, Benjamin
Listed as a Private on Muster Roll of Capt. Peter Ruton's Company in the 4th. Battalion of New Jersey Volunteers commanded by Lieut. Col. Abraham Buskirk (Bushkirk) at Staten Island in May and July (Deserted) 1778.
Source - DSR

TWITCHEL, John
Listed as Private in muster roll of Capt. Christopher Hatch's Company of Loyal Americans, commanded by Col. Beverly Robinson at Haarlem, New York, possibly at beginning of 1778 and again on 21 April 1778.
Source - DSR2

VAN CORTLAND, Philip
Listed as an Ensign on Muster Roll of Capt. Peter Ruttan's Company in the 4th. Battalion of the New Jersey Volunteers commanded by Lieut. Col. Abraham Buskirk Esq. (place unknown) and possibly dated Jan. 1779. He was listed as on leave on Long Island, New York and is listed again at Governor's Island on 29 Oct. 1779 (not joined?) and on Dec. 1779 muster. Also on 19 March (listed as just Cortland) and May 1780 muster. On 14 July and 11 Sept. and 2 Dec. (absent with leave) 1780 muster at Staten Island, New York, on leave on Long Island, New York. Listed on 29 April 1781 muster at Staten Island.
Source - DSR

VANDYKE, John Major
Granted with other refugee loyalists (21), 380 acres of land by Governor Parr on 8 August 1795 (85?) in Kings County, Nova Scotia, Canada.
Source - HKC#3

VANGESEA (Vangeser), Samuel
Listed as a Sergeant on Muster Roll of Capt. Peter Rutton's Company in the 4th. Battalion of New Jersey Volunteers commanded by Lieut. Col. Abraham Buskirk at Staten Island, New York on 30 Dec. 1778. Also listed in Jan. 1779 Muster (location unknown).
Source - DSR

VAN GIEZEN (Vangesen), Samuel
Listed in Muster Roll of Capt. Peter Ruton's Company in the 4th. Battalion of New Jersey Volunteers commanded by Lieut. Col. Abraham Bushkirk at Staten Island, New York in May and July (listed as Carpenter) 1778 as a Sergeant. Again listed on Muster possibly dated August or September and October 1778 and on command in New York. On March 1779 Muster at Hobuck (Hoboken), New Jersey and at Powles Hook 7 July 1779 and again in August 1779, sick in the barracks and listed again at Governor's Island on 29 Oct. 1779 and Dec. 1779. Also on muster 19 March and May 1780 (location unknown). On 14 July and 11 Sept. (sick) and 2 Dec. (Orderly with General Patterson)1780 muster at Staten Island, New York. Listed on muster 29 April 1781 at Staten Island.
Source - DSR

VAN ORDEN, William
Listed in 4th. Battalion New Jersey Volunteers muster roll commanded by Lt. Col. Abraham Bushkirk and Capt. Peter Ruton (Ruttan) at Staten Island, New York dated March 1778. Listed as a Private and dead. Also listed as a Sergeant on 18 Nov. 1777 Muster at same place. He enlisted on 7 Dec. 1776. Listed again as a Sergeant on 6 Jan. 1778 Muster at same place, but deceased on 8 Dec. 1777.
Source - 4BNJVM & DSR

VAN SLYKE, GERARD
From Tryon County, New York near the Mohawk river and was the tenant to Col. Claus. Taken prisoner in April 1780.
Source - HP

VAN SLYKE, Jacobus
From Tryon County, New York near the Mohawk river and was the tenant to Sir John Johnson. Taken prisoner in April 1780.
Source - HP

162 *The New Loyalist Index 3*

VAN SYLE (Sile) (Zyle), John
Listed as a Private in Capt. Peter Ruton's Company in the 4th. Battalion of New Jersey Volunteers commanded by Lieut. Col. Abraham Buskirk (Bushkirk) at Staten Island, New York in May and July (Sick) 1778 and possibly on August or September and October and 30 Dec. 1778 Muster at same place. Listed again on Jan. 1779 Muster (location unknown). On March 1779 Muster at Hobuck (Hoboken), New Jersey and at Powles Hook 7 July 1779 and on August 1779 muster in same Company and at Governor's Island on 29 Oct. 1779 and Dec. 1779, on Furlow. Also on muster 19 March and May 1780 (location unknown). On 14 July and 2 Dec. 1780 muster at Staten Island, New York. Listed on 29 April 1781 muster at Staten Island.
Source - DSR

VAN VOLKENBURGH, Isaac
Listed with Sir John Johnston's Brigade and later joined Butler's Rangers. Disbanded in 1783 and possibly was granted land in Niagara, Ontario.
Source - SJJB

VEALY, Baltus
Listed as Private on muster roll of Capt. John Howard's company of New York Volunteers commanded by Lieut. Col. George Turnbull Esq., Commandant at Paulus Hook, February 1778.
Source - DSR3

VERDON (?), John
Listed as Private on muster roll of Capt. John Howard's company of New York Volunteers commanded by Lieut. Col. George Turnbull Esq., Commandant at Paulus Hook, February 1778.
Source - DSR3

VOUGHT, Christopher
Granted with others 8,900 acres 15 Oct. 1784 by Gov. Parr in Kings County, Nova Scotia.
Source - HKC#2

VOUGHT, John Capt.
Listed in Gen. Skinner's Brigade, Seconded Officers (date unknown) at age 37 from America.
Source - GSB

VOUGHT, Joseph Capt.
Granted with others 8,900 acres by Gov. Parr 15 Oct. 1784 in Kings County, Nova Scotia.
Source - HKC#2

WAGER, Allen
Late of Sussex County, New Jersey, listed 9 Feb 1779 at Sussex Court of Inquiry by Isaac Martin and Samuel Meeker, Commissioners.
Source - NJNE

WALKER, Daniel
Listed with Sir John Johnston's Brigade and later joined Joseph Brant's Volunteers. Disbanded in 1783 and possibly granted land in Niagara, Ontario.
Source - SJJB

WALKER, Peter
Listed as Private, working as a Tailor at Harlem on muster roll of Capt. John Howard's company of New York Volunteers commanded by Lieut. Col. George Turnbull Esq., Commandant at Paulus Hook, February 1778. Again on muster of Capt. William Gray (same company) from 24 Feb. to 24 April 1781, location unknown.
Source - DSR3

WALKER, Richard Esq.
Granted with other refugee loyalist's 21, 380 acres by Gov. Parr 8 Aug. 1795 (85?) in Kings County, Nova Scotia. Excheated 14 May 1814.
Source - HKC#3

WALLIS(?), John
Listed as Private in May 1783 Muster Roll of Lieut. Col. Stephen Delancey, commanded by Col. Cortland Skinner Esq. at New Town (location unclear).
Source - DMR

WANNAMAKER (Wannemaker), Conrad (Connrate)
Listed in 4th. Battalion New Jersey Volunteers muster roll commanded by Lt. Col. Abraham Bushkirk and Capt. Peter Ruton (Ruttan)at Staten Island, New York dated March 1778. Was listed as a Private killed on 1 March 1778. Also listed on 18 Nov. 1777 Muster at same place. He enlisted on 22 Jan. 1777. Other listings are 6 Jan. 1778 (same place).

Source - 4BNJVM & DSR

WANNAMAKER (Wandemaker), Derick
Listed in 4th. Battalion of New Jersey Volunteers muster roll commanded by Lt. Col. Abraham Bushkirk at Staten Island dated March 1778. Was listed as a Private and was captured and placed in jail in Philadelphia, Penn. where he died in 1780. Wife was Elizabeth who later married John Post and settled with other loyalists at Maugerville, New Brunswick, Canada. Also listed on 18 Nov. 1777 Muster at Staten Island, New York. He enlisted on 7 Dec. 1776. Other listed are dated 6 Jan. 1778 (same place) as sick in quarters. Again in March and May and July (Sick on Staten Island) 1778 Muster at same place.
Source - 4BNJVM & DSR

WANNAMAKER (Wannemaker), Henry (Henery)
Listed in 4th. Battalion New Jersey Volunteers muster roll commanded by Lt. Col. Abraham Bushkirk and Capt. Peter Ruton (Ruttan) at Staten Island, New York dated March 1778. He was listed as a Private held prisoner by the rebels. Also listed on 18 Nov. 1777 at same place as taken prisoner on 29 Dec. 1776. He enlisted on 7 Dec. 1776. Again on 6 Jan. 1778 Muster at same place and still a prisoner. October 1778 Muster at same place says; enlisted 6 Dec. 1776, taken prisoner 20 Dec. 1776, returned 2 Oct. 1778 with note; Not subsisted nor received bounty. Listed again on 30 Dec. 1778 Muster at same place. Listed again on Jan. 1779 Muster (location unknown). On March 1779 Muster at Hobuck (Hoboken), New Jersey and at Powles Hook 7 July 1779 and again on August 1779 muster in same Company and at Governor's Island on 29 Oct. 1779 as sick in camp and on Dec. 1779 stating he "Has not drawn his bounty, Furlow". Also on muster of 19 March and May 1780 (location unknown). On 14 July and 11 Sept. 1780 muster at Staten Island, New York. On 2 Dec. 1780 muster at Staten Island, New York he is noted as being "on board Sloop Neptune".
Source - 4BNJVM & DSR

WANNAMAKER (Wanmaker), John
Listed in the 4th. Battalion New Jersey Volunteers muster roll commanded by Lt. Col. Abraham Bushkirk and Capt. Peter Ruton (Ruttan)at Staten Island, New York dated March and May 1778. He was listed as a Private held prisoner by the rebels. Also listed on 18 Nov. 1777 Muster at same place as taken prisoner on 29 Dec. 1776. He enlisted on 7 Dec. 1776. Again on 6 Jan. and July and possibly August or September 1778 Muster at same place and still prisoner. October 1778 Muster at

same place says; enlisted 6 Dec. 1776, taken prisoner 20 Dec. 1776 and returned 2 Oct. 1778 with note; Bot subsisted nor received bounty. Listed again on 30 Dec. 1778 Muster at same place. On March 1779 Muster at Hobuck (Hoboken), New Jersey and at Powles Hook 7 July 1779 and again on August 1779 muster in same Company and at Governor's Island on 29 Oct. 1779 and Dec. 1779 stating he "Has not drawn his bounty, Furlow". Also on 19 March and May 1780 muster (location unknown). On 14 July 1780 muster at Staten Island, New York. Listed on 29 April 1781 muster at Staten Island.Source - 4BNJVM & DSR

WANNAMAKER, Nicholas
Listed in the 4th. Battalion New Jersey Volunteers muster roll commanded by Lt. Col. Abraham Bushkirk and Capt. Peter Ruton (Ruttan) at Staten Island, New York dated March and May 1778. He is listed as a Private held prisoner by the rebels. Also listed on 18 Nov. 1777 Muster at same place as taken prisoner on 29 Dec. 1776. He enlisted on 7 Dec. 1776. Again on 6 Jan. and July and possibly August or September 1778 Muster at same place and still prisoner. October 1778 Muster at same place says; enlisted 6 Dec. 1776, taken prisoner 20 Dec. 1776, returned 2 Oct. 1778 with note; Not subsisted nor received bounty. On 30 Dec. 1778 Muster, same place and on Jan. 1779 (location unknown) as a prisoner. On March 1779 Muster at Hobuck (Hoboken), New Jersey and at Powles Hook 7 July 1779 and on August 1779 muster, but taken prisoner on 19 Aug. 1779 and at Governor's Island on 29 Oct. and Dec. (Has not drawn his bounty) 1779 still prisoner. Also on 19 March and May 1780 muster (prisoner)(location unknown). On 14 July and 11 Sept. and 2 Dec. 1780 muster at Staten Island, New York (prisoner). Listed on 29 April 1781 muster at Staten Island (prisoner).
Source - 4BNJVM & DSR

WANNAMAKER, Peter
Listed in the 4th. Battalion New Jersey Volunteers muster roll commanded by Lt. Col. Abraham Bushkirk and Capt. Peter Ruton (Ruttan) at Staten Island, New York dated March 1778. He was listed as a Private held prisoner by the rebels. Also listed on 18 Nov. 1777 Muster at same place as taken prisoner on 29 Dec. 1776. He enlisted on 7 Dec. 1776. Again on 6 Jan. 1778 Muster at same place and still listed as prisoner. October 1778 Muster at same place says; enlisted 6 Dec. 1776, taken prisoner 20 Dec. 1776, returned 2 Oct. 1778 with note; Not subsisted nor received bounty. Again on 30 Dec. 1778 Muster, same place. On March 1779 Muster at Hobuck (Hoboken), New Jersey and at Powles Hook 7 July 1779 and again as a Corporal on August 1779 muster with

same Company and at Governor's Island on 29 Oct. 1779 and Dec. 1779 stating he "Has not drawn his bounty". Also on muster 19 March and May 1780 (location unknown). On 14 July and 11 Sept. 1780 muster at Staten Island, New York.
Source - 4BNJVM & DSR

WANNAMAKER, Richard
Listed in note on muster roll of 4th. Battalion New Jersey Volunteers commanded by Lt. Col. Abraham Bushkirk and Capt. Peter Ruton at Staten Island, New York dated March 1778 that he died in jail in Philadelphia, Penn. in 1780. Listed as a Private on possibly August or September and October Muster Roll 1778 at Staten Island, New York. His widow, Elizabeth remarried to John Post and they settled at Maugersville, New Brunswick, Canada. Richard is listed again on 30 Dec. 1778 Muster at Staten Island, New York as on guard, and again on Jan. 1779 Muster (location unknown) as prisoner. On March 1779 Muster at Hobuck (Hoboken), New Jersey and at Powles Hook 7 July 1779 and again on August 1997 muster, noted that he was taken prisoner on 19 Aug. 1779 and at Governor's Island on 29 Oct. and Dec. 1779 still prisoner. Also on 19 March and May 1780 muster (prisoner)(location unknown). On 14 July and 11 Sept. and 2 Dec. 1780 muster at Staten Island, New York (prisoner). Listed on 29 April 1781 muster at Staten Island (prisoner).
Source - 4BNJVM & DSR

WARD, Edmund Capt.
Granted with other loyalist refugees 21,380 acres by Gov. Parr 8 Aug. 1795(85?) in Kings County, Nova Scotia.
Source - HKC#3

WARD, John
Listed as Lieutenant on muster roll of Capt. Christopher Hatch's Company of Loyal Americans, commanded by Col. Beverly Robinson at Haarlem, New York, possibly at beginning of 1778 and again on 21 April 1778.
Source - DSR2

WARD, Moses Lieut.
Granted with other refugee loyalist's 21, 380 acres by Gov. Parr 8 Aug. 1795 (85?) in Kings County, Nova Scotia. Excheated 14 May 1814.
Source - HKC#3

WARNER, Levi
Of Claremont, New Hampshire claims he served with the British during the entire war and was at St. Johns at the head of Lake Champlain in 1783. Says he joined Burgoyne during Fall of 1777.
Source - NHL

WATT, Frederick
Listed as Private on muster roll of Capt. William Gray's company of New York Volunteers from 24 Feb. to 24 April 1781, location unknown.
Source - DSR3

WEAVER, Peter
Listed as Private and confined with the Rebels on muster roll of Major Thomas Barclay's company in the Loyal American Regiment commanded by Col. Beverly Robinson at Guanus on 11 May 1782.
Source - DSR2

WEBB, George
Listed as a Private on Muster Roll of Capt. Peter Ruton's Company in the 4th. Battalion of New Jersey Volunteers commanded by Lieut. Col. Abraham Buskirk (Bushkirk) at Staten Island, New York in May and July and possibly August or September, October and 30 Dec. 1778. Listed again in Jan. 1779 Muster (location not given) as a Sergeant. On March 1779 Muster at Hobuck (Hoboken), New Jersey and at Powles Hook 7 July 1779. Listed again as a Sergeant in August 1779 in same Company and at Governor's Island on 29 Oct. 1779 and Dec. 1779. Alson on 19 March and May 1780 muster (location unknown). On 14 July and 11 Sept. and 2 Dec. 1780 muster at Staten Island, New York, sick in quarters. Listed on 29 April 1781 muster at Staten Island.
Source - DSR

WEBB (WEBBS), Nehemial
From Sandwich, Barnstable County, Massachusetts (Cape Cod). Was a mariner. Was a POW in 1779. Banished, left but came back for a short time. Listed as prisoner in Boston and was allowed to return to Sandwich to finish his affairs and leave in 1779 (TM3 p.80/2). He was listed as a Captain allowed parole to visit his family per the Sandwich Town Meeting. He was part of the Tory underground on Cape Cod and met at Seth Perry's house (see his listing) with other loyalists.
Source - DH & LMTOS & SA

WEBB, William
Listed on muster roll of Lieut. Col. John Connolly's Corps of Loyal Foresters, commanded by Capt. Alexander McDonald, taken at Hellet's Cove, Long Island, New York 28 Aug. 1781 listed as a Private. Possibly became a refugee in unit #3 who came to Saint John, New Brunswick on the ship, Hopewell with four other family members in 1783. This same person could have been the William Webb, age 84 who died around August 1814 in Saint John, New Brunswick, Canada. He was the Keeper of Alms House in that city.
Source - RF

WEBB, William
Listed as Corporal on May 1783 Muster Roll of Lieut. Col. Stephen Delancey, commanded by Col. Cortland Skinner Esq. at New Town (location unclear) (not sure if below listed William is the same as this one?)
Source - DMR

WEEKS, Henry
Listed as Private, working as a Tailor in Harlem on muster roll of Capt. John Howard's company commanded by Lieut. Col. George Turnbull Esq., Commandant at Paulus Hook, February 1778. Also on muster of Capt. William Gray (same company) from 24 Feb. to 24 April 1781, location unknown.
Source - DSR3

WELCH, Thomas Sargent
Listed on muster roll of First Battalion of Maryland Loyalist 11 July 1778 at Long Island, New York. Enlisted on 6 Nov. 1777.
Source - ML

WENTWORTH, Benning (Gentleman)
Followed Gov. John Wentworth to Flatbush, Long Island, New York (not sure of relationship). He later returned to Nova Scotia after the war and was given several high offices, member of council, secretaryship and treasurer of the Province between 1795-97. New Hampshire General Assembly listed him and 75 others as the enemy in Nov. 1778. His home was at Portsmouth, NH. Listed on act of confiscation 28 Nov. 1778.
Source - NHL

WENTWORTH, John Gov. Esq.
Governor of New Hampshire took his family to Fort William and Mary at Portsworth Harbor for safety and later fled on the British ship, Canso on 24 Aug. 1775 with the Captain of the Fort, John Cochran to Boston and remained there until March 1776 where they went to Halifax, then to Philadelphia, then to London on 13 March 1778. He did spend a time at Flatbush, Long Island, New York. There, in Jan. 1777 he writes a letter to his sister telling her of the conditions of other Portsmouth refugee's who were following him, as Meserve, Hale, Lutwyche, Capt. Cochran, Macdonough and Benning Wentworth. Listed as an enemy Nov. 1778 and as from Portsmouth, N.H.. Listed on act of confiscation 28 Nov. 1778. From England he went to Halifax, Nova Scotia 20 Sept. 1783 and became the Surveyor General of all the King's woods in Nova Scotia at a pay of L800 a year. He spent the following 8 years protecting the royal preserves for the building of ship masts. The now, Sir John and Lady Wentworth lived at Prince's Lodge near Halifax. They went back to England in 1810 and 1811. Sir John died 8 April 1820 at 84.
Source - NHL

WESTBROOK, Anthony
Listed on land grant petition with others 12 July 1793 to John Graves Simcoe, Esq. for land located between Long Point and Turkey Point on the west side of Lake Erie.
Source - EGRS

WHEATON, Caleb
From Sandwich, Barnstable County, Massachusetts (Cape Cod). Was a gentleman who was banished. He was part of a Tory underground who met at Seth Perry's house (see his listing) for a loyalist meeting.
Source - LMTOS & SA

WHEELER, John
Listed in 4th. Battalion New Jersey Volunteers muster roll commanded by Lt.Col. Abraham Bushkirk and Capt. Peter Ruton (Ruttan) at Staten Island, New York dated March 1778. Listed as Private and discharged.
Source - 4BNJVM & DSR

WHIT, John
Listed in New Jersey Volunteers muster roll commanded by Col. Joseph Barton and Capt. James Shaw dated 26 Jan. 1777.
Source - NJM

WHITE, John
Heirs granted 500 acres in Rawdon/Douglas, Nova Scotia under Major General Small.
Source - WWRD

WHITEL(?), John
Listed as a Private on May 1783 Muster Roll of Lieut. Col. Stephen Delancey, commanded by Col. Cortland Skinner Esq. at New Town (location unclear).
Source - DMR

WHITING, Benjamin Esq.
From Hollis, NH. The New Hampshire General Assembly list him and 75 others as the enemy in Nov. 1778. Was listed on muster roll of Corps of Volunteers associated with New Hampshire loyalist Gov. John Wentworth at Flushing, Long Island, New York on 16 Oct. 1777 as a First Lieut..
Source - NHL

WIGHTMAN, John Lieut.
Granted with others 8,900 acres 15 Oct. 1784 by Gov. Parr in Kings County, Nova Scotia.
Source - HKC#2

WILBORNE (Wilbore)(Wellbore), Joshua
From Sandwich, Barnstable County, Massachusetts (Cape Cod). Was a gentleman and banished and left the state. Was part of the Tory underground and met at Seth Perry's house (see his listing) with other loyalists.
Source - DH & LMTOS & SA

WILDRIDGE, James
From Falmouth, Maine or Massachusetts? Was a mariner. Wife was Elizabeth. Cumberland County, Massachusetts's property was forfeited in 1782. Was banished to Canada.
Source - DH

WILKESON, (?)
Listed as Private in May 1783 Lieut. Col. Stephen Delancey, commanded by Col. Cortland Skinner Esq. at New Town (location unclear).
Source - DMR

WILKESON, George
Listed on muster roll of First Battalion of Maryland Loyalists 11 July 1778 at Long Island, New York. Enlisted 6 Nov. 1777.
Source - ML

WILKINSON,........... Private
Granted land 13 Dec. 1785 in Douglas, Nova Scotia for service in 2nd. Battalion, 84th. Regiment.
Source - WWRD

WILKISON (Wilkeson), John
Listed as a Private on Muster Roll of Capt. Peter Ruttan's Company in the 4th. Battalion of New Jersey Volunteers commanded by Lieut. Col. Abraham Buskirk Esq. (location unknown) in Jan. 1779 as with the Southern Army. (He could be one or both of the above?) and at Powles Hook 7 July 1779 Muster and again on August 1779 muster and at Governor's Island on 29 Oct. 1779 and Dec. 1779 stating he in "On ye Detachment". Also on 19 March 1780 (location unknown), but "On Expedition with The Commander in Chief" and again in May 1780 with General Clinton. On 14 July and 11 Sept. and 2 Dec. (with southern army) 1780 muster at Staten Island, New York listed as "On Southern Expedition". Listed on 29 April 1781 muster at Staten Island, but noted that he was with the Southern Army.
Source - DSR

WILLARD, Levi
A gentleman from Charlestown, NH. The New Hampshire General Assembly listed him and 75 others as the enemy in Nov. 1778.
Source - NHL

WILLARD, Solomon
A gentleman from Winchester, NH. The New Hampshire General Assembly listed him and 75 others as the enemy in Nov. 1778.
Source - NHL

WILLIAMS, Abraham
Listed as Private on muster roll of Capt. Christopher Hatch's Company of Loyal Americans, commanded by Col. Beverly Robinson at Haarlem, New York, possibly at beginning of 1778 and again on 21 April 1778.
Source - DSR2

WILLIAMS, David
Listed with Sir John Johnston's Brigade and later joined Joseph Brant's Volunteers. Disbanded in 1783 and possibly granted land in Niagara, Ontario.
Source - SJJB

WILLIAMS, Ekbert
From Tryon County, New York near the Mohawk river and was the tenant to Sir John Johnson. Taken prisoner in April 1780.
Source - HP

WILLIAMS, Elijah Esq.
Fled from Keene, New Hampshire after the battle of Lexington. The New Hampshire General Assembly listed him and 75 others as the enemy in Nov. 1778. List on act of confiscation 28 Nov. 1778. Was listed as a Second Lieut. in the Corps of Volunteers associated with New Hampshire Loyalist Gov. John Wentworth at Flushing, Long Island, New York on 16 Oct. 1777. He was on a petition 20 Feb. 1784 to change Conway to Digby, Nova Scotia, after Rear Admiral Robert Digby. Around 1784, he went back to Keene, NH to transact some business and was caught and placed before the court of sessions at Charlestown. He was order to leave the State which at that time returned to Nova Scotia. He became very ill and again returned to Deerfield, New Hampshire where he died.
Source - NHL

WILLIAMS, Jacob
Listed as Private on muster roll of Capt. John Howard's company of New York Volunteers commanded by Lieut. Col. George Turnbull Esq., Commandant at Paulus Hook, February 1778.
Source - DSR3

WILLIAMS, Stephen
Listed as Private on muster roll of Capt. Christopher Hatch's Company of Loyal Americans, commanded by Col. Beverly Robinson at Haarlem, New York, possibly at beginning of 1778 and again on 21 April 1778.
Source - DSR2

WILLOUGHBY, William
Listed with Sir John Johnston's Brigade and later joined Joseph Brant's Volunteers. Disbanded in 1783 and possibly granted land in Niagara, Ontario.
Source - SJJB

WILLOUGHBY, William
Listed as loyalist settler in Cornwall, Ontario in 1790's alone and on his land.
Source - LCO

WILLSON, Benjamin
Listed on land grant petition with others 12 July 1793 to John Graves Simcoe, Esq. for land located between Long Point and Turkey Point on the west side of Lake Erie.
Source - EGRS

WILSON, Francis
Listed as Private on muster roll of Capt. John Howard's company of New York Volunteers commanded by Lieut. Col. George Turnbull Esq., Commandant at Paulus Hook, February 1778. Again on muster of Capt. William Gray (same company) from 24 Feb. to 24 April 1781, location unknown.
Source - DSR3

WILSON, Samuel Capt.
Granted with other refugee loyalist's 21, 380 acres by Gov. Parr 8 Aug. 1795 (85?) in Kings County, Nova Scotia.
Source - HKC#3

WINDECKER, John
From Tryon County, New York near the Mohawk river and was the tenant to Col. Claus. Taken prisoner in April 1780.
Source - HP

WING, William
Listed as Private on muster roll of Capt. William Gray's company of New York Volunteers from 24 Feb. to 24 April 1781, location unknown.
Source - DSR3

WINTER, William
Listed in 4th. Battalion New Jersey Volunteers muster roll commanded by Lt. Col. Abraham Bushkirk and Capt. Peter Ruton (Ruttan) at Staten Island, New York dated March 1778. He is listed as a Private held prisoner by the rebels. Also listed on 18 Nov. 1777 Muster at same place as taken prisoner on 29 Dec. 1776. He enlisted on 7 Dec. 1776. Again on 6 Jan. 1778 Muster at same place and still prisoner. Again in March and 30 Dec. 1778 Muster as prisoner and Jan. 1779 (place unknown). On

March 1779 Muster at Hobuck (Hoboken), New Jersey and at Powles Hook 7 July 1779 still listed a prisoner with Rebels and again on August 1779 muster and at Governor's Island on 29 Oct. and Dec. 1779 still a prisoner. Also on 19 March and May 1780 muster (location unknown). On 14 July and 11 Sept. and 2 Dec. 1780 muster at Staten Island, New York (still prisoner). Listed on 29 April 1781 muster at Staten Island (prisoner).
Source - 4BNJVM & DSR

WINTERMUTE, Peter
Late of Wyoming (Penn.?), but listed in inquisition 9 Feb. 1779 at Sussex County, New Jersey at Court of Inquiry by Isaac Martin and Samuel Meeker, Commissioners.
Source - NJNE

WINTERMUTE, Philip
Late of Wyoming (Penn.?), but listed in inquisition 9 Feb. 1779 at Sussex County, New Jersey at Court of Inquiry by Isaac Martin and Samuel Meeker, Commissioners.
Source - NJNE

WIRE, Thomas
From Falmouth, Maine or Massachusetts? Possibly stayed after British left.
Source - DH

WOOD, Caleb
Listed as Private on muster roll of Capt. Christopher Hatch's Company of Loyal Americans, commanded by Col. Beverly Robinson at Haarlem, New York, possibly at beginning of 1778 and again on 21 April 1778.
Source - DSR2

WOOD, John
Listed in Cornwall, Ontario but removed to Carleton Island 1790's.
Source - LCO

WOOD, Jones
Listed in Cornwall, Ontario 1790's as loyalist settler.
Source - LCO

WOOD, Stephen
Listed as a Private in May 1783 Muster Roll of Lieut. Col. Stephen Delancey, commanded by Col. Cortland Skinner Esq. at New Town (location unclear).
Source - DMR

WOOD, Thomas
Listed as a Private who deserted on Muster Roll of Capt. Peter Ruttan's Company in the 4th. Battalion of New Jersey Volunteers commanded by Lieut. Col. Abraham Buskirk Esq. (location unknown) in Jan. 1779. Listed again on 2 Dec. 1780 muster at Staten Island, New York.
Source - DSR

WOOLER, Joseph
Late of Sussex Co., New Jersey. Listed in inquisition 9 Feb. 1779 at Sussex Court of Inquiry by Isaac Martin and Samuel Meeker, commissioners.
Source - NJNE

WOOLVERTON, Thomas
Late of Sussex County, New Jersey, listed in inquisition 9 Feb. 1779 at Sussex Court of Inquiry by Isaac Martin and Samuel Meeker, Commissioners.
Source - NJNE

WOOLY(?), Elisha
Listed as Corporal in May 1783 Muster Roll of Lieut. Col. Stephen Delancey, commanded by Col. Cortland Skinner Esq. at New Town (location unclear).
Source - DMR

WRAP, Coenrad
Listed in 4th. Battalion New Jersey Volunteers muster roll commanded by Lt. Col. Abraham Bushkirk and Capt. Peter Ruton (Ruttan) at Staten Island, New York dated March 1778. Listed as Private and discharged.
Source - 4BNJVM & DSR

WRIGHT, Alexander
Listed as Private in May 1783 Muster Roll of Lieut. Col. Stephen Delancey, commanded by Col. Cortland Skinner Esq. at New Town (location unclear).
Source - DMR

WRIGHT, Ebenezer
Listed as loyalist settler in Cornwall, Ontario alone in 1790's, but recorded as going back to the States for his family.
Source - LCO

WRIGHT, John
From Falmouth, Maine or Massachusetts? Was a merchant. Banished and left the state.
Source - DH

WRIGHT, William
Listed as Private on muster roll of Major Thomas Barclay's company in the Loyal American Regiment commanded by Col. Beverly Robinson at Guanus on 11 May 1782.
Source - DSR2

WYNG, William
Listed as Private on muster roll of Capt. John Howard's company of New York Volunteers commanded by Lieut. Col. George Turnbull Esq., Commandant at Paulus Hook, February 1778.
Source - DSR3

YELVERTON, Thomas
Granted with others 8,900 acres 15 Oct. 1784 by Gov. Parr in Kings County, Nova Scotia.
Source - HKC#2

YOUCKER, Jacob
From Tryon County, New York near the Mohawk river and was the tenant to Sir John Johnson. Taken prisoner in April 1780.
Source - HP

YOUNG, Christopher
Listed in New Jersey Volunteers muster roll commanded by Col. Joseph Barton and Capt. James Shaw dated 26 Jan. 1777.
Source - NJM

YOUNG, Philip
Listed in 4th. Battalion New Jersey Volunteers muster roll commanded by Lt. Col. Abraham Bushkirk and Capt. Peter Ruton (Ruttan) at Staten Island, New York dated March 1778. Listed as Private and discharged.
Source - 4BNJVM & DSR

YOUNGLOVE, Ezekiel
Late of Sussex County, New Jersey, listed in inquisition 9 Feb. 1779 at Sussex Court of Inquiry by Isaac Martin and Samuel Meeker, Commissioners.
Source - NJNE

ZIMMERMAN, Matthias
Listed in New Jersey Volunteers muster roll commanded by Col. Joseph Barton and Capt. James Shaw dated 26 Jan. 1777.
Source - NJM

www.ingramcontent.com/pod-product-compliance
Lightning Source LLC
Chambersburg PA
CBHW072131160426
43197CB00012B/2061